MW01135458

# Before Language

Poems by

## SUSAN DEER CLOUD

Before Language

Copyright © 2016 by Susan Deer Cloud

All rights reserved. No part of this book may be reproduced or transmitted in any form or by any means without written permission of the author.

Back cover photo of Susan Deer Cloud & Beat Stähli by John Gunther

Back cover photo: "Spirit to Spirit" (Beat Stähli's hand holding hand of his sculpture)

Bio photos of Susan Deer Cloud by John Gunther

Front cover photo: Beat Stähli's sculpture titled "The Source"

Library of Congress Control Number: 2016943997

ISBN: 978-0-9915772-2-4

Published by Shabda Press
Pasadena, CA 91107
www.shabdapress.com

# Acknowledgements

With sincere gratitude to the editors and publishers who included some of the poems in *Before Language* in the following literary journals and anthologies: *Comstock Review; Sin Fronteras; Earth's Daughters; Oddball Magazine; Verse-Virtual; Yellow Medicine Review; Tell Tale Inklings; About Place Journal; Rat's Ass Review; I Was Indian (Before Being Indian Was Cool) Native Anthology; The Border Crossed Us (An Anthology to End Apartheid); WPFW 89.3 FM Poetry Anthology; Nuclear Impact, Broken Atoms in Our Hands Anthology; Unraveling the Spreading Cloth of Time: Indigenous Thoughts Concerning the Universe Anthology; Women Artists Datebook 2016.*

Thank you, nya'weh, to the mystery writer, Elizabeth George, and the Elizabeth George Foundation, for giving me the grant that set in motion the still continuing journey that resulted in this book ... and to John Gunther who drove me all across America, Europe, and what I call the Magical Isles, when this poet can't comprehend "stick shift" and may well have been overwhelmed by driving on the left side of Great Britain's and Ireland's roads not to mention on Germany's Autobahns. If our roving were a road movie we might well title it "Driving Ms. Susie." John, Raised-by-Wolves, you're a real prince.

To my publisher and editor, beloved poet Teresa Mei Chuc ..... Cảm ơn bạn from my soul to yours.

Last, but certainly not least, Danke to the brilliant wood sculptor, Beat Stähli, for agreeing to have his wood carving, "The Source," grace the front cover of *Before Language*. My heart soars like an eagle.

# The Poet's Preface

*Before Language* has more beginnings than I could ever have imagined when I began writing down the mystery of what seeded it into word constellations longing to speak light from the original stardust of my very atoms. The astronomer, Sir Arthur Eddington, once said, "Not only is the universe stranger than we imagine, it is stranger than we can imagine." I and countless others of the creator tribe bow enthralled to the universe within us and encircling us, compelled to express that *je ne sais quois* at the core of why we write, paint, sculpt, carve, compose music, and dance. No matter if the rest of the world mocks us as fools, often leaving us weeping and poor, singing like vivid canaries in any number of mine shafts about to blow. Our art is our primary love, a perennial passion and constant love-making that metamorphoses us from mere fools into holy fools spouting crazy wisdom. If ever there existed eternal love, such love is embodied by the solitary ceremonies of our creating. For me, it is as if what I call the Great Mystery flames through my fingers shape-shifting into eagle wings, soaring as poems onto the skies of page upon page. I could no more stay away from my writing than Juliet could keep away from her glorious Romeo.

*Before Language* crystallized when I was given an Elizabeth George Foundation Grant in January 2013 in response to my application requesting money to travel in Ireland where I wished to seek its pre-Christian culture that bore deep resemblance to Turtle Island Northeast/Southeast Indian cultures. As with many people in the Catskill Mountains and Appalachia, I am of Indian, Irish, Scotch-Irish and other Isles lineage (and so much more). Whatever made us so, well, *hot* for each other?!! Little did I guess that this plan of mine was about to take me on a journey that still has not ended, first cross-country in America and up to Canada, and twice to Europe. During the summer I traveled cross-country with my roving companion, John Gunther, I got the results of mitochondrial DNA-testing I had done. Upon reading them, I burst out laughing, for evidently my ancestresses going back to that first mother in Africa had the same wanderlust I was born with. Where hadn't my ancestresses roamed to? That evening John and I were camping out in Utah, surrounded by red rock. For this "Red Indian," so far from her other ancestral homes on the far side of two vast oceans, it seemed as if that rock lit to fire by the setting sun symbolized the myriad mother layers of my ancestresses' lives leading up to me, the fool poet. Entering further into my wandering both in North America and abroad, I realized that I had unwittingly entered into trying to solve a mystery, the mystery of transient self but also of what any one human being is in all of her or his complexity. How perfect when the grant that provided passageway into this splendid adventure was provided by an extraordinary writer of mysteries, Elizabeth George.

I am most fond of the Japanese prosimetric form, haibun, which describes a person making a physical journey naturally becoming a journey of the heart/mind. This odyssey invariably leads to a haiku, a flash of epiphany appearing after the memoir/story/essay part of the haibun. This instant of transformative insight into what the journey signifies in the deeper ways is much like that point where one halts for the most stunning view when hiking up a high mountain. It is that lingering in which there is no longer any need for human words, the timeless moment of "When you speak *It* is silent. When you are silent *It* speaks." During these past years' travels I was fortunate to experience many such moments that rendered me speechless. Each was a Blakean "Eternity in an hour" that my poetry and stories can only point to, the junctures where mere human words risk forcing something vastly beautiful into something undeservedly small.

I and all contemporary human beings dwell in an unsettling era of over-population, climate change, increasing divisions between rich and poor, cheap diversions for concealing any truths, the Forever War, and mass migrations of desperate men, women and children. My recent "magical mystery tour" and the meanderings of my entire existence have been to bring attention to the nitty-gritty of others' lives, bear witness to their and my realities, and to write those complexities down in a singing 3-d language. I try to keep what I observe in balance and record not only tragedy but goodness and gladness. I am intrigued by how people turn hardship and struggle into dreams, continuing kindness, and healing gentleness despite having been kicked around, put down, and kept down. As I write this, America, my beloved Turtle Island, is mired in a civil war in which millions of betrayed citizens are rising up and calling for a revolution. How many times has this story been repeated throughout human history? The so-called millennials sound the way I and my sisters and brothers of the 1960s and early 1970s sounded when we took to the streets *en masse* and similarly cried for a revolution that would bring us "love, not war." What children we were. And, yet, "out of the mouths of babes" may be what a world gone mad needs to hear. I pray that the sweet passion of the lovers prevails and the toxic heartlessness of the haters fails.

During my journey I made a pilgrimage to Brienz, Switzerland, the Heimat (home region) of my Swiss great grandmother, Lina Stähli, who emigrated when she was eighteen to join her brother, Fritz, in America's Catskill Mountains. After John parked our car just outside the village, we strolled beside the lake into Brienz, stopping to gaze through the generous windows of a woodcarver's studio. A book on art by Hermann Hesse leaned jauntily against a sculpture we were marveling over; next we noticed the name Beat Stähli on a card taped to the door, along with an email address and phone number. Nearing Christmas, this was the greatest gift I could have received, for the woodcarver shared my great grandmother's maiden name *Stähli* and apparently shared my fondness for the writer, Hermann Hesse! But the door was locked, and this artist who I suspected was my relation could only be glimpsed in his brilliant carvings. Following upon that sunny afternoon in Brienz, which included hiking up a trail to an Alpine waterfall and spotting eidelweiss and blue lupine blooming in late December, we emailed Beat who graciously invited us to return and meet him in the back of his atelier. And so we met, embarking upon "the beginning of a beautiful friendship" in that sunny room facing Lake Brienz and the loveliest valley in Switzerland. I felt as if I had borne my great grand-mother Lina's broken heart back home inside my own scarred heart, that pretty orphan girl who I learned may have been sent away with welfare money from her Heimat. I consoled myself by reflecting that she at least moved to other wildflower-dotted mountains, the Catskills I grew up in. The delicate white edelweis blooming in Brienz's unusually warm winter became the symbol of a Swiss émigré returning after more than a century.

The day I met Beat and saw more of his wood sculptures I hoped that one of his carvings would grace the cover of my next book. He kindly agreed to this but explained the sculpture I chose was fashioned after Rodin's "Danaïd" and should be acknowledged as such. Acknowledged. Only for me, Beat's Danaïd sculpture embodied in a lone female the stories of all my ancestresses through the mitochondrial-DNA line of my maternal grandmother, her mother, Lina Stähli, all the way back to our original Dreamer Mother. For me, the sculpture conjured up other ancestresses, as well. Certainly I could glimpse intense sorrow in that burnished basswood figure bowed to the ground, her long hair like a river of tears spilling into the mute dirt, yet I also perceived the immense sensuousness, tenderness, and exquisite vulnerability required for any human being to experience pure love and ecstasy. I understood that Beat had made love to wood with his sensitive hands, evoking the interior spirit of a tree with his holy fire, liberating the passion, love, grief, dreams and wandering of myriad women of many countries and centuries in that nude anything but wooden in spirit. I wept upon seeing her sepia blaze because she and hence Beat made me feel no longer so lonely.

In this afraid world longing for sanity, may any readers who hold *Before Language's* woman and poetry in their wistful hands also no longer feel so lonely.

x

*Before Language* is dedicated to


my kindred spirit, Beat Stähli, and his sister now my little sister, Manuela ...

Jim Curtis a.k.a. "Just Jim," Anam Cara, brother of the Thunderbird ...

&

all those brave people who have held to the Beauty Way in a crazy world.

\* \* \*

# Contents

# PART I

"I want freedom, the right to self-expression, everybody's right to beautiful, radiant things."

Emma Goldman

# First Body

The first body was a boy
in dormer window high
on third floor of an old house
whose paint had chipped away
to grey scars among white.
The first body ... a mountain boy
whose father had "that old time religion,"
thumping his black Bible across town,
shouting "Repent, sinners," warning
mountain pagans about the fires
of hell. The first body blazed
solitary in summer sun rays,
bending over as if to tie a shoe.
The first body ... boy verged
on becoming a man,
slender, silent, luminous
in its bowing more powerful
than prayer. The first body ...
and ten year old Indian girl
gazing up from dandelion lawn
in awe. The window boy
with whip scars ... wondering
if the father would punish him
that night just for having flesh.
The first body naked as dawn
by torn lace curtain ...
the shy girl with hazel eyes
escorted by butterflies.
Bodies like halos.

# Opal's (for Aunt Pat & Uncle Lou)

Aunt Pat calls after our New Year flowers
reach her and Uncle Lou's Long Island house
countless roads and highways distant from
this Catskill town she and I grew up in,
then fled as soon as we could ...
two Libra girls riding love to places
big enough for our dreams.

She can't see my smile when she describes
the deep purple of the glass vase, purple
my lover kept shaking his head over
when I asked him to order *that bouquet*
"because it color-coordinates with those
purple wampum roses among the callas" ...
me laughing at his Capricorn confusion,

"I'll never understand this thing about
coordinating colors," him making his stand
in paint-stained blue pants and orange shirt.
Yes, Aunt Pat calls and tells me gaily
how she has centered the flowers
on a table of things with similar colors,
oh, we daughters of Venus know how

to bring life into balance even in January.
Happily we reminisce about earlier times,
the girls we were, the people who were,
remembering her mother and father,
my grandparents who lived right next door.
Aunt Pat conjures up summers
Grandma worked for Irving Berlin ...

when dinner became Grandpa
strolling with her to Opal's place
by the railroad tracks, tossing her high
up on the bar, inquiring grandly,
"What will you have to drink, Pat?"
"A glass of beer!" she'd sing out,
and of course everyone there

cheered the darling with her
deer eyes and wildflower face
that would make a calla lily appear
like a mere weed. Outside
what little snow this winter brought
sparkles in the year's new light
like fire opals. Window-lit

I recall when Aunt Pat married
a Libra man who carried her off
the way every good prince does ...
think how opal is our birthstone,
so softly white with elusive
hues. So easily cracked.
But she and I speak little today

about all that makes us break,
our ache of voices reaching
for the old gaiety of us before
we grew old. We don't mention
blue-eyed Louis, her firstborn,
who died last July, nor her
Parkinson's or Uncle Lou's

cancer. Instead, we go for
a joyride back to Grandma
"who was always gentle," and to
Grandpa who used to lift his jewel
of a daughter on Opal's bar, a star
to admire. Aunt Pat, I also want a beer …
to toast such love that never dies.

# Veterans Day, Old Pictures

Some Veterans Days I look at
old pictures of my father, cupping
sepia or Kodak black-and-white
to my hands' heart and fate lines
broken before I was even born
to a Daddy wounded in the
"Good War," that handsome
fresh meat in Marine uniform
who fought on Vella Lavella,
months later was shot on Guam.

Other Veterans Days I gaze
at nothing, if lucky
in a place where I can't hear
a parade or feel my heart shake
from military drums and trumpets,
or have taps tear into my ears,
hurting more than politicians'
speeches like islands of clichés.
The nothing days hurl me
back to the nights before

pictures, to the little girl
lying still as a corpse in bed,
her father crying out
from nightmares on the other
side of the wall he painted
pink as the lip of that big

conch shell he found
on some beach, a soft color
for me he dreamed would have
freedom forever, never war.

In the few photographs
from my father's young years,
there exist no pictures of 3 a.m.
screams or the fragments
my mother spoke, "Malaria,
pleurisy, night sweats, safe
now, get you cooled down,"
his horrors and her attempts
at healing until their voices ebbed
and I could lift my head in hope

that my Daddy would stay alive.
None of the Kodak images show
twin round scars on his chest
and back, white as binary stars
from where the Japanese sniper's
bullet hit him sprinting through
surf onto Guam's coral beach,
impossible to dig foxholes in.
The pictures were as quiet
as he was about the battles,

never one to brag about fighting,
a man who told me just once,
"I was stupid about war when I
joined the Marines, so young
my immigrant parents had to

sign for me eager to keep
their new country free."
No 1940s snapshots show
Marines jammed together,
sweating in a boat nearing Guam,

"We didn't speak, we all knew
most of us would be wounded
or dead before the day ended."
Veterans Day again approaches,
trees shed leaves three weeks past
October first, date my father
was hit by a heart attack at fifty-one.
"The family doctor said the wound
would shorten his life by twenty years,"
my mother confided. I kissed his

forehead where he lay in a coffin,
still as I once lay, embalmed skin
hard as coral. I was twenty four.
A boy played taps, a second echoed,
when our Marine was lowered into
a hole in a mountain graveyard.
My three brothers, sister, Mom and I
cried while trying to bury our faces.
On Veterans Day I might look at photos
of him before he decided to be brave.

# Vietnam War Story

He wasn't like that before Vietnam.
He didn't want to fight. He didn't want
to kill anyone. He was drafted. Poor
small town boys had no way to escape
the draft. They sent him into the jungle
where women were fighting for the
Vietcong. Women captured by his unit.
His sergeant shoved one of them
towards him, yelled "Shoot her!"
He said he wouldn't do it, he didn't
believe in killing. "Oh, yeah?"
The sergeant raised his pistol,
pressed it to his skull. "Believe
or I'll shoot you." He wasn't
like that before he shot the woman
with eyes whose silence was louder than
the sergeant's yelling and never stopped
screaming after she dropped in a heap
to the jungle floor. She wasn't the only
female Vietcong they caught that day.
There were daughters, too. Brains,
blood, everywhere. So if you
wonder how he robbed and killed
an eighty year old woman when he
returned to the States, went to prison
then after his release helped murder
another woman because she wouldn't
give him and his buddies money

and her car, that's how. That's why
he could run that "fat white trash" over
with her beat up Ford nine times.
"I remember him when they first
let him out," I released my pent
breath. "Swaggering down Main Street,
smack in the middle as if he were
going to whip out two pistols
and have a shootout at high noon.
My mother started laughing, said
he looked like he had a load in his pants.
How could they set him free again
after he killed another country woman?"
No clue. I see him wandering
by the rivers. He's mellow.
We always say "Hello."

# Atoms (for Erelene)

Every weekday on the far side of town
my sister eight years younger than I
wakes to her alarm's pre-dawn buzz,
barely able to move because her body
hurts in every atom and her neck,
once broken, locks up.

Every darkest hour, five days a week,
she wakes this way the same as our father
once woke, shaking off a dreamtime
sometimes tortured with nightmares,
the same as women and men all across
America wake and instantly want

to weep because they must go to work
at some shit job for little pay (everyone
knows if you complain you get fired).
Everyday my sister awakes in the bedroom
where I first saw her, newborn,
in my mother's arms, 1959

right before the 'Sixties made the scene
and we all felt hope again, believing
people really could soften life's meanness,
stop wars like "The Good War" our father
was wounded in, prevent poverty,
racism, sexism, dismantle

the nuclear bombs. I marched against
the Vietnam War and for the poetry
of good causes because I didn't want
my baby sister to ever cease smiling
the way she smiled that January evening
I bowed my face over her eyes

completely blue, irises
and even the "whites."
I wanted life to blaze
like the sky of her eyes for her,
to bring Peace and Love,
not the worries I had because

I heard my father cry out in the nights,
the bullet repeatedly entering his chest,
because I had my own nightmares
after air raid drills at school
and the Bay of Pigs when we feared
the Soviets would soon drop

the atom bomb on Manhattan,
a prime target and us only
a hundred miles away sure to die
of radiation. Every weekday
my sister groans out of bed,
limps stiffly to a cold kitchen,

brews coffee then sits outside
to watch the sun rise effortlessly,
leaving a trail of roses above
the east horizon. Yesterday
she phoned when she dragged home
from work, wept she was afraid

there'd be a nuclear holocaust after
the latest Taliban beheading and Putin
making bare-chested threats. I consoled her
until we white-haired sisters renewed
our vow to forever see roses
in a newborn sky blue on azure.

# Crones Against Drones

In this winter people call old-fashioned
our hair grows long with blue icicles ...
snow glints through nights as though
sky were Lady Day, snowflakes
gardenias falling from her hair.

Back in these Catskills
we crones hunker down in,
one can almost return to a past
in which Earth dreamed deep
beneath snow-beguiled days,

children flashing by
on sleighs and skating so fast
they turned into little birds.
In those moons lit to fire opals
across the drifts, the children

could trust they were safe
and spring green in time.
Not like this 21ˢᵗ century where
we old women notice how few
girls and boys go outside

to play away from video games
and TVs droning behind locked
doors. And we wonder
if the games teach children
to accept politicians' droning

lies, and radio-controlled drones
sent to kill and spy in the name
of saving American lives.
"Bug splats" they call the drone
dead, including the collateral

damage of exploded children
once like our sweet mountain kids
before they retreated inside.
We crones of creation
are regarded the same

as this old-fashioned winter,
our hair like the snowy twigs,
our hearts like ice jams,
making others uneasy
because we don't drone

but speak fierce as nor'easters.
We who remember how to hibernate
with bears and be as bird children
awaiting winter crocuses
to sing through snow.

# Windows

Not computer Windows but high paned windows
brighten classroom's far wall on Career Day ...
and I the poet invited back to hometown school
to speak about a "writer's career"
feel sad for Catskill students squeezed
behind tiny desks pointed away
from windows I used to daydream through,
wondering where I might rove, who meet,
in a future of wandering over horizon lines
until my atoms could dance with Pacific sunsets.

Not a chance of "getting off topic" here, no
distractions except for a teacher's "on track" hand
writing math formulas across white board,
the urging to pay attention or get detention. Except
I who suffered through geometry two years in a row,
refusing to do it, playing hooky, going on picnics
and skinny dipping instead of taking finals,
ask students to look towards the windows
allowing in this day's hopeful February sun, snow
sparked to blue diamonds, gentle Catskill rises

transcending square walls and learning the angles.
Yes, I speak about windows, not just those
leading to the world and universe outside,
but the interior windows of the human heart,
mind, soul, call it what you will, of never turning
one's back on what is eagle-soaring free, life lit

by the sun and moon of passion and dream.
Poet who grew up country, poor, "part
Indian," proud outcast metamorphosing
on the inside of mystery, I marvel

I was once like these teenagers approaching
manhood and womanhood, poised to be licked
into shape by love's metaphorical mother bear
until formed enough to taste the honey of experience.
"White hair" that I am, old fool faithful
to poetry, I don't want that girl with sparkles
in her purple hair to cease dancing, that boy
doodling to relinquish his fingers' visions,
nor the dreamcatchers of so many tender faces
to forget how to let only the good dreams in.

# Skinny Dipping in the Willowemoc

When she goes skinny dipping
in the Willowemoc, in old
swimming hole few people
still know, she floats

with breasts gleaming wet
in sunshine redolent of 1960s ...
Catskill "flower child"
who once swam with lovers

long haired and naked as she,
doing the breast stroke towards
each other to see how it felt
to fuck like fish, becoming

rainbow trout *coming*
in cold sparkles mirroring
shore trees until greener
than her eyes closed in

ecstasy. Now when she
skinny dips in the river
with an Indian name,
she enters alone

into the Willowemoc,
glimpses indigenous ghosts
who left behind the word
hiding a lost story,

sees her "half breed" mother
who stoically snapped
together her white cotton bra
each morning, forgetting

ancestresses who lived
bare breasted through summers
and didn't grow suicidal
or get breast cancer ...

Beauty who never
learned to swim or dared
to grow hair long
like her green-eyed daughter.

# At the Bottom of the Stairs

At the bottom of stone stairs ...
garden and gold forsythia
planted by the woman who
dwelled there.

But those few who *knew*
knew she was a wife dying there,

and after slaps and punches
that left her face a hurricane sky
greenly darkening

she planted sprigs
of forsythia at the base
of stairs

her husband dragged her
by her long braids
down. Fast

her forsythia grew, spread
like the crazy years.
Gowned and mute
she pruned

branches trying to rise up
over Gloucester wall,
bush first to bloom
in spring.

That forsythia
men poets call gold
was never gold,

and yellow now glows
unpruned and free

as the woman's ghost
who barefoot strays
beyond the walls by Cripple Cove.

# After Tassia's Funeral, Toledo, Ohio

After Tassia's funeral we rode back
with Barbara and Alan to Victorian house
trimmed in blues, black cat on porch
where the Black Swamp once was.
Drained, its shadows had sheltered
Barbara's Seneca ancestors when they ran
to hide, hungry, in the sloughs of long snakes,
much as my people escaped into Catskills
that John and I had left the day before.
Mourners drained as the swamp ...
we women seeing ancestresses
flash like invisible foxfire. No, it is

not right for a daughter to die
before her mother and father, tragic
her own daughter is left motherless,
the shining one I call Sparkle Girl ...
unspeakable how the scent of Tassia's hair
clings to the pillow next to her husband's,
no river-bathed body or Bear Clan spirit
accompanying it like a flute awaiting
the lover's enlivening breath. We gather
nearly breathless, Indians and Jews ...
behind us centuries of practice in swallowing
down screams and tears, yes, screaming
grief is what I want to do, but

we each sink into our usual Black Swamp
of grief felt in lost languages and pilfered
dreams. I manage to say that John and I
saw a bald eagle and twin fawns sporting
velvet antlers when yesterday we headed out ...
eagle gliding over river, fawns emerging
in flecked awe from forest glistening with dawn.
*Maybe some kind of good sign? Maybe*
*eagle and deer conveying what we can't say?*
We sip wine the tint of blood, talk between
silences, finally drag to bed, falling off
to sleep as if we, too, had dropped
dead at Strawberry Moon end.

# Coyotes, Catskills

Others in her half-emptied town
don't hear them as she does …

coyotes up past old cemetery
Great Uncle Fred called
Boot Hill. She knows
that mountain well, cave

created by tumbled
down boulders,
blackberry patch,
a meadow whose tall
grasses and daisies

lovers found refuge in
when life still pretended
to be innocent.

In 1950s and '60s
no coyotes howled
two, three hours past
midnight. No cat-eyed
humans listened

while prowling across
a dreamscape glinting
with tongue-tied stars.

These mountains had become
like that Round Top graveyard ...
gone the coyotes, wolves, bears,
eagles and egrets.

And the Indians lay low,
wordless as the ghosts
of the disappeared
mammals and birds.

Once, though, she heard
a panther scream in the forest
behind the house
her Native grandpa
built to shelter his family.

She figured those wild beings
were forced to flee and hide
same as her Indian family
hid and played dead.

Panther cried
someday they would all
come out. Her own scream
silent ...

*I will wait.*

# The Price of Peeing at the Iroquois Musuem

… Two hundred miles of coffee-drinking making your bladder
howl. You veer off Route 88, figure you'll use Iroquois Museum
Ladies Room outside Cobleskill, NY. Mohawk, this Museum
is one of your homes away from *never quite feeling at home*
in colonial America. Besides, relatives claim Chief Tiyanoga,
misnamed King Hendrick, was your ancestor. On visits,
you stand before his portrait, track down any possible resemblance.
Like him, you always have a strange wolf at your side …
ready to fight for your people until someone ambushes you
from behind. You sigh, brake, pray you can ride the eloquent
horses of warrior words the way that Mohawk orator
rode them into old age. Late April day. How happy you feel,

dashing through the door. How sweet entering into
memories of long ago before First Contact, skin petaled open
to cherry and apple blossom scents mingling with Chanel # 5,
Libra self-indulgence, last curtain call of feminine luxury.
Lips smile like a pink blossom at young woman selling
entrance tickets, "Mind if I use the Ladies Room, browse
in the shop? Too late to wander through the Museum."
She frowns above brown ribbon shirt, "You need to pay
eight bucks. Ladies Room is in the basement. That means
you'll walk through the Museum." No pun intended, I'm pissed.
"Whoa, I just have to pee! I've been to this Museum many times.
I won't peek, promise. I'm Mohawk. We get to pee for free."

"Okay, keep your voice down, there are other people here."
"Where?" I ask in my Peacemaker's voice that at its loudest
wouldn't make a skunk spray. It's true, I've done my research.
"All I see are ghosts and you treating me like one." She sulks,
"I'm Mohawk, too. Go. Use the Ladies. Just don't look at anything."
I flash her my Sky Woman smile of an entire fruit tree blooming
wild at high noon. I fancy dance to the Ladies Room, void, then *look*.
I look at my face with eyes leafed out to green fire. Looking more,
I brush my long silver hair, touch poet's fingers to prayer braid,
then sneak silkily in ankle-length skirt to Chief Tiyanoga trapped
in paint. I gaze at dreamer's face until he gifts me the red blanket
over his shoulders. I bound upstairs with clan wolf, slip
my Red spirit past young woman interfacing with computer
behind official Haudenosauee desk. We the People of the Longhouse.
Eight bucks to pee at our Museum of a Once Generous People.
Or if you blaze with tomahawk tongue ... your free but broken heart.

# How We Find Each Other
## (for Paul Hapenny)

The Chinese, for instance, believe the universe
unfolds in patterns repeating themselves over and over
like picture chants. When I was smarter than I am now
and used to read Nietzsche, I learned how he spoke
of "eternal return" before the syphilis left him
infinitely mad. And just between you and me,
once when I was cleansing my "Doors of Perception"
I glanced in the mirror and plunged into Eternity, seeing
my many forms shining back to the innocent naked one
in the first Garden … barring the Buddha who kept floating
from my heart, only manifestation that never changed.
You should know I have been a Mohawk medicine woman,
French cancan dancer, German whore, and ancient
Chinese poet who reappears more than all others.
And no doubt I have been rainbows, snow crystals on pines,
and for that matter horseflies on shit, slugs and bugs.

So tonight this thing I call my *self* is breathing inside
its current sac to keep whatever mystery it is all in,
pretending solidity, while wondering about you, Friend,
how we found each other. I can entertain any possibilities
in this strange cosmos. At first I thought it was our poetry,
then figured it was the Indian or Irish blood. Soon
your voice taught me we share patterns reaching far back.
Perhaps you who say you are an atheist would laugh
at any notion that we as patterns keep weaving together
through millions of years. Maybe I should laugh at the notion

of a Native atheist, even though I once spoke as you do,
could no longer believe in God and tried to kill myself
when I was twelve. You know, I died then, and dying
can teach a "mixed blood" child what really is sacred and of
love and worth. Dear friend of crazy brilliant stories, this ghost
saw you that long ago mescaline day through the looking glass.

# Delete

You glance at wall clock hands
clicking to midnight ... February 13th,
day your mother died. Full moon
following Saturday's blizzard
collapses through windows like blank
sunlight after your mother slipped
from cancer coma into death.
Flat light, no warmth ...
you, your sister, and brothers
wrapping arms around each other
in mute circle, relieved your mother
had finally died.

That blank light transporting you
twenty years back to the hospital when you
tried to grant your mother's last wish,
to *die at home* ... to breast cancer blasting
into her vertebrae, to surgeon who scolded,
"Your mother can't return to the mountains
unless she agrees to wear a halo brace."
That fall you stopped being just a daughter,
crashed into a new identity when the surgeon
hustled you aside to brag weirdly,

"Your mother is pretty. Pretty women always
get their way. But she can't manipulate me
because without a brace her neck will break.
No, she won't break *me*." You glanced at
hospital clock, stared at the specialist's clock-like
face, numerical eyes, summation that you, too,

were pretty … your auburn hair tumbling down
around your shaking body, your cat eyes, slant
cheekbones and full mouth that you knew could
suck the arrogance out of his antiseptic bones.
Shaking more, you raised your shy voice,
"She's my *mother*. She's *terrified*. You told her
you'd put screws in her skull to hold the brace in."

February 13th again, recalling that poem
you wrote following your mother's cremation …
words wanting to punch the surgeon's face in
because then he'd know when you grow up poor
and rural and Indian it doesn't matter how *pretty*
you are, doesn't matter how fucking beautiful
and brilliant and witty and brave,
all you ever will be to most people
is penniless, invisible, it's the American
nightmare that will keep you dying like that.
Then he'd know how it feels, *how it doesn't feel*,
to wander faceless on Mother Earth.

But the professor you eventually divorced
urged you to delete your rage, *too strong*, readers
might take the poem *wrong*, think it *anti-man*,
*anti-American*. You glance at wall clock hands
ticking towards another frozen dawn. You
have never ceased feeling your mother's hands
weakly holding yours after the bald doctor drilled
screws into her head. Your pretty mother
still wearing Evening of Paris, her skin
like tonight's moonlight …

and you, her daughter,
battling to keep beauty
from being deleted forever.

# Mixed Blood (for Dorothy Little Sparrow)

I am tired of you who condemn me
and others for being "mixed blood"
as if you were a surreal breed of Red Aryans
when you are merely Indians with BIA cards
and reservations that started as nothing
more than concentration camps,
those camps Hitler based his on.

I am sick of your colonized crap,
of making excuses for you
self-anointed warriors, male and female,
thinking you can attack an old woman poet
because you believe her too weak, sweet,
or fearful to fight back. But I don't
fear cowards who define others

based on blood, skin and hair color,
cards that spell defeat, divide-and conquer
laws used to keep still free Indians
from calling their art Native American,
don't get that casinos are the antithesis
of our old and beautiful ways.
You Indian cops who killed Sitting Bull,

know this elder makes a stand
against betrayers perpetuating
U.S. genocide against US. As I told
my youngest brother once, I am proud
to be a woman of many lineages,
it shows my people are not racists
when it comes to love, indicates

we embody our Iroquois Tree of Peace
inviting all people in (wink), says
our ancestors ignored the borders of hate.
"Oh, sure," my brother laughed,
"it probably just means we're oversexed."
Mixed blood Indian love medicine,
no wonder the sellouts get jealous of sexy me.

# Jug in Desert

Her man drove their Subaru
from Big Bend summit down
Chihuahua Desert road
hardly a road, not yet solstice
but June heat close to 100 degrees
and the Sun of No Clouds burning
across eyes, creosote bush, and cacti
flaming forth an occasional unsure
flower. Nothing like desert blooms,
miniature oases of rose or yellow
in hundreds of miles of baked
dirt. She learned quick not to squat
and pee in those desert places,
splashed up unlike in northern woods.
And in ladies' rooms perched atop
Chisos Mountains campsite,
black scorpions waited at every door.

*I'm starting to see how those*
*desert nomads conjured up*
*that Old Testament God*
*who would smite you dead*
*the way a scorpion will a mouse.*
*Had I been an ancient wanderer*
*I might well pray and beg for mercy,*
*even inside this car I feel afraid.*
They had read about the dreamers
sneaking across the border,

decided to visit the Rio Grande
and maybe wade through river
the other way. But once there
they could not bear the vengeful sun
on their New York skins,
retreated to air-conditioned car.
They waved to a Mexican family
having a picnic on cottonwood bank,
smiled at barefoot boys riding
unsaddled horses through
the muddy freedom water.

Her man drove them back
on even less traveled road,
faint wheel tracks on sand and rock.
They wanted to see for themselves
that Texan desert where people
stole across man-made border
to become *aliens* in the country
stolen from Indians like her.
*You know, a lot of them are really*
*indigenous, so what do I care if they*
*join us sisters and brothers up north?*
Then she fell mute, speaking
only when her man had to stop
for some arroyo washout,
the two of them rushing to pile rocks
in order to drive on. After
hours of jouncing over earth
so seemingly dead that even
a scurrying mole gave cause
for joy, they spotted a plastic

gallon jug along the road
hardly a road. Half emptied
of water. *There are those*
*who leave water jugs for the ones*
*who make it across the Rio Grande*
*then run north through desert.*

And that idiot cliché snaked through
her thirsty brain, *The optimist*
*sees the water glass half full,*
*the pessimist half-empty.* She tried
to view the jug as half-full, tried praying
to the Big Daddy of desert places
Nietzsche had pronounced dead,
*Please let whoever drank from the jug*
*be alive, please, O God, let them*
*survive like surprise desert flowers.*
She had read about the lovers' bones
gleaming below desert stars, and the raped
corpses no longer dreaming of green cards.
Two hours later they passed Panther Junction
onto paved road prowling up to camp
where later they would make love
and cry.

# I Can't Breathe (for Eric Garner)

Eric, I grieve you are no longer here
to even breathe the word "I" … tall vowel
so many Black men have struggled
to inhabit. I think I understand
about wanting to be shown respect,
I, Catskill Mountain Indian who bears
stories about bullies who tried to strangle
my spirit and sacred breath.

Like you, Eric, I have suffered
from asthma, panic of wheezing
little deaths that can crescendo
to a last gasp. I cried when I watched
those videos of you being harassed by cops
outside Staten Island beauty supply store,
know how it feels to beg "Don't touch me,"
saw that young uniform choke and choke
you, shocking your face down into hot

hard sidewalk while you pleaded for life.
No beauty supplied there, and those
who keep lying it wasn't murder
kill you and your smile again and again.
I wept when your daughter, Erica,
pressed her body down in the night
during protests following Grand Jury
dismissal of your latter day lynching …
Erica, who will try forever to breathe
inside that place of her father's dying.

Six children left behind, no Big E to play
Santa Claus this year, no "Gentle Giant"
cradling youngest daughter born last spring.
Finally in death a tall "I" … Mr. Eric Garner.

# I Was Sitting with My Friend

I was sitting with my friend, Ras Charles, by the Confluence
of the Chenango and Susquehanna Rivers, when he told me
about his brother. Early April ... sunning on a bench,
a little chilled, Charles dressed in his usual Rastafarian fashion,
dreadlocks flaming down past his shoulders and across bright
clothes. He told me about his brother's addiction to drugs
and about the woman who wanted to get Valium from him ...
how she stabbed the brother with an ice-pick, not once
but many times until she was sure he was dead
and she could steal his drugs. Ras Charles, who looms way
over five feet two me, started crying. I wrapped my arms
around him, but barely, his shoulders like the hills' horizon.
I rocked and cradled his body. After a while he stopped,
choked "I'm sorry." I soothed, "Please don't apologize.
I only wish I could bring your brother back."
Then he spoke about black men, including the mothers
so strict with their sons, afraid they might dance out
into the white world and make a misstep. "Goes back
to slave days and post-Civil War days of lynching
black men for just pretty much being alive," he sighed.
A white woman strode close by, squinting at us ...
Middle America to the max, with stretch pants, stretch
belly, short dyed permed hair, and the American flag
waving in her Fox News-eyes. No missing the rage
in her face. One of the ugliest faces with the most hate
I had ever seen in my life. I said nothing to Charles.
I didn't think he saw, his own eyes shivering again
with tears. But I knew what *she* saw, or thought she saw,

what word was polluting her brain, the N-WORD,
*that N* being embraced by someone she thought was white
because I am a mixed lineage Indian with light skin.
Yes, and *that old hippie* because I wear long skirts,
beaded earrings and uncut hair like Ras Charles, holy
hair. I wrapped my arms tighter around him, rocked
him and hummed to him until the woman stomped away
from the place where the Indian-named rivers touch to flow
into one another, the sacred place of my long ago ancestors
massacred there. The valley for drying tears.

# Alberta Hunter, Tonight
# I'm Thinking of You

Alberta Hunter, tonight I'm thinking of you ...
maybe because first fall tinges the cooling
air, rain playing a soft Blues across roof
and earth waiting for the trees' annual
striptease. *'Round about midnight*
I am listening to you on old LPs,
newer CDs, and videos, Alberta,
on YouTube. Tonight in my study
in the misty mountains, you remind me
I'll be 65 come late October when
leaves shimmy off twigs, transforming
frost-silvered lawns to shards of rainbows
cut loose ... my limbs a winter tree
in an America that prefers spring.

Alberta, my sister promised there will be
a birthday party in honor of my growing
old. I grin about how you pulled that
off, still flaming forth in your eighties,
insinuating sex mated to Blues while
gyrating pelvis saucily under
sundown blue dress. And, yes,
despite *My Handy Man Ain't Handy*,
those moves weren't ever for a man
but for your longtime woman lover.
No use in catching the Blues from men ...
including your father who abandoned
you and your Mama in 1895 Memphis,
when you were born.

I guess a black girl whose mother
had to work as a maid in a brothel,
a half orphan who ran away at 11
to Chicago, cleaning saloons until
she got a gig singing at Dago Frank's,
another whorehouse ... soon
supporting her mother while keeping
the female lover a secret ... learned plenty
about the Blues without any husband's help.
No one ever sang *Nobody loves you*
*when you're down and out* that jaunty
way you wept it without tears. At 65
may I acquire your smile, Alberta,
more beguiling than the Mona Lisa's.

# Black Girl with No Name (for Sarai)

A night I just wanted to watch an old movie ...
safe in bed while outside the full moon
made it appear as though snow sparkled over
Earth rather than pre-Halloween ghost-light.
Channel surfing, I paused on CNN video
of huge Caucasian cop slamming a black
girl out of classroom chair, flipping her
upside down, desk banging to floor along
with soft body, dragging splayed arms
and legs to the door. When a second
black girl started crying in protest,
the "resource officer" yelled "Sit down
or you're next!" Stunned, other students
made secret videos in the "shock and awe"
South Carolina school. And what would I
have done about that goon with a gun?

Speaking of *doing*, what did the black girl
with no name do? Briefly text someone?
Nothing I saw on the videos justified her
being tossed about, a mute rag doll
like that day my ex yanked my hair and body
to kitchen floor, neck snapped into whiplash.
Will the high spirited schoolgirl descend
into years of pain, a nervous breakdown,
flashbacks forever more?  In trauma
so deep she nearly forgets she has a name
or tears to shed?  Last night I thought

about the little Cherokee-Black girl
who lives in the house across the street ...
girl magical, courteous, sweet,
who makes me smile whenever she speaks
of dance lessons, puppies and stars.

October 27 ... ghosts glimmering near,
daylight growing less, skies more bruised.
Come Halloween when the little girl sashays
up to our porch in her princess way
and lilts "trick-or-treat," I give her
a black cat bag, a cornucopia
of candies and rainbow ice pops,
a wand with a glow-in-the-dark star,
a stuffed puppy with immense eyes ...
my way to say *May no bully ever*
*grab you by the hair. May no fascist*
*drag you into forever fear.* Last zombies
disappeared, I pray Grandmother Moon kisses
the faces of Sarai across our street, the nameless
black girl, and the one who cried.

# It Don't Matter, Election Day 2014

Not that I can't remember being young and a rebel,
only in the days of Civil Rights, anti-War, Women's Rights,
Gay Pride and American Indian Movement marches
I was a rebel with a cause believing everything mattered.
I, unable to vote at 18, feel shocked by 21$^{st}$ century youth
crowing they won't vote. "Why?" I chant. "Why?"
And they can only croak, "It don't matter." But I,

moved back to Catskill hometown after decades
of living hither and thither and roving in between,
walk to Town Hall to cast my mid-term election vote.
Maybe these young ones become like the mountains,
valleys, rivers, caves. What need have *they* for civic duty?
Later I'll learn 60 percent of Americans felt no need,
even women once deemed not smart enough to vote.

On election day this mountain Indian woman
thinks of the young man at Peck's Grocery,
boy-man with that frayed half-washed appearance,
hunger leaving a low dying fire in his eyes,
sinkholes in a face forever drooping towards torso
in worn flannel, ubiquitous clothing in these parts.
I offered to let him go ahead at the checkout,

him with just hot dogs and Pepsi in his hands.
He smiled a little, "It don't matter," his voice
low, sad, haunted, haunting, and carefully polite
in a way that made me want to cry. On election day

I am thinking of the girl who came trick-or-treating
Halloween Eve, garbed in 19th century clothes,
fulsome body shy inside homemade dress,

girl at border between childhood and womanhood.
I am hearing her lilt "It don't matter" when I asked
if she wanted chocolate bars, Dots, or ice pops.
Something in her saying of it made me want
to give everything I had, she half-whispering
"Thank you" for the Dots as if she had received
rubies, emeralds and topazes … me wondering

about her story hidden by ankle-long dress
of wildflowers like dresses I once wore
and still wear. If only I could hug her
with such kindness it would begin to matter,
and she would see she was a star, the queen
of lynx-eyed spirits … she of the moon face
lacking Halloween mask, her face itself a mask.

On election day I recall the privileged One Percent,
the spawn of the rich, entitled prep school kids,
the snots who call country people "rubes," "rednecks"
and worse. To those arrogant, clever, sarcastic
and cynical, I say your soullessness "don't matter."
On election day I cast my defiant vote, my hope
it will matter for the beautiful hopeless once more.

# The Moon Wears a Red Dress (for Justin)

September 27, 2015, many of us awaited
the lunar eclipse, I in Catskills praying
predicted rain would not sheer across mountains
before my beloved and I could watch full
moon whirl behind and closer to Mother Earth
until shawled by shadow. As usual

the night mountains appeared like silhouettes
of animals' and lovers' bodies, air redolent
with last asters and goldenrod, first
falling leaves. We kept stepping out
on upstairs deck like an eagle's aerie.
At last it began in air still mostly clear …
smudge of eclipse, bit by bit the Moon
waning through her phases in a brief time.

"Look, oh, look," we sang back and forth
beneath bejeweled rarity of shadow
making love to reflected light …
Moon my Iroquois People call
Grandmother now garbed in
softest scarlet. My mate trilled
he was going down to Dubois Street
to watch the rest, I following

to behold sunrise and sunset
become one in Super Blood Moon's
shy hue. Silent there in empty road

I remembered a photograph of red
dresses hanging in a Canadian woods,
bearing witness to indigenous women
murdered or gone missing.
Only other person watching ...
young African-American man
who dwells across from us, smiling
up at Grandma Moon who loves
that night sky of black skin.

Soon rain clouds gusted in,
and the eclipse itself grew
eclipsed by mist in lunar
peekaboo. Indian woman waning
to 65, in blood red poncho
I danced with ghosts.

# Aunt Maude's Last Love

By then her cataracts had cascaded so thick
across her eyes she was blind except for
an occasional glint of light. By then
she'd been a decades-long widow,
her oldest son, the crazy one, had just
died, and the younger took her at last
to a nursing home after the old grey house
accumulated stories that could qualify
as Northern Gothic. Before the move
my sister stopped by, stripping Maude
so she could wash crusted shit off
her legs and thighs, days of it because
the sons left her crumpled on a couch
in a room with shades always drawn.

By the time I visited Aunt Maude
in the nursing home, she was her fierce
self again, demanding my sister and I
sneak her through a window and drive her
far back into Catskills where she could
hide. Her red hair had flamed out
to white found only in mountain winters,
snow unsullied. She couldn't see
my sister and me grin when she pushed
herself up from the wheelchair,
face thinned to all Indian cheekbone,
lips like hatchet blades.
We relived with her the happy days
when she went out dancing and men
banged their guitars and howled for her.

That's where "Honey," as she called him,
came in, the young aide with café au lait skin
and voice that sounded like her endearment.
Whenever Honey spoke, her lips parted
into a flirtatious smile, dimmed
eyes managing to glow again until
their former hazel flashed forth,
fragile flesh flush with girlish giggles.
He sang for her, too, honky-tonk
love songs like slow dance kisses …
that African American Honey
with skin mirroring softly the night
in Aunt Maude's eyes. Her evening star.

# The Suicide of the Moon

She didn't talk about it, but ever since 1969
when that strange metal thing lowered itself
onto her and the bubble-headed creature
emerged with its umbilical cord and jumped
her in slow motion, she felt depressed.
Not your "once in a Blue Moon" blues,
no, this was every day and every night
desiring to die.

No one noticed. Most of the world
celebrated her violation and the metallic
creature who gloated triumph. That world
she had mirrored light for cheered as
"One small step for man, one giant leap
for mankind" beamed through space
into billions of ears. It is true
some leftover Romantic poets cried,

but certainly in America no one
much paid attention to their lunar light.
Also, a bunch of Turtle Island Indians
got upset, like the Iroquois who called
the Moon "Grandmother" ...
weeping Indians right down there
with the poets on the social scale.
So she marveled when that same August

half a million young people
dressed up like Indians and artists
to create "Woodstock," the greatest
music festival that ever was.
But hadn't she always been
the glowing symbol of "Peace/Love"?
Yet no hippies flashed peace symbols
up at her invisible in the rain.

The rape really got to her.
Love isn't very good at fighting
back. She only knew how to hang out
in space and inspire the sensitive ones.
She was just an old Grandma
waning. The poets lost interest
in her. The Indians went off to college
and learned she was a lump of stone.

# I am Lonely for My Loneliness

I am lonely for my loneliness on this
Strawberry Moon when fireflies mirror
the stars, Great Bear dipping down like a bow
to those solitary ones awake past midnight,
universe fur-black in hibernations of dreams
glimmering back to the Big Bang. 2 AM,

and I am lonely for the loneliness
of losing my mother and father, for being
an outcast after my second divorce,
for becoming an aging poor poet woman
trying to keep her pride and not let
"the respectable" see her cry on a rotting

floor in Rod Serling's hometown,
Twilight Zone of skeleton factories
and old loony bin on outskirt hill flinging
lunar shadow across the long valleys
of muddy rivers. On this last bursting
of Strawberry Moon, so flush with rose

you'd never imagine that men once jumped
on the face of what we Iroquois call our
Grandmother, I am lonely for living man-less,
for dwelling with Persian cat before she died,
for holing up with her in third floor garret
and reaching far down into the holy fire

of my once sweet heart battered to ash,
hoping for a spark to bring my own new
universe into wonder. I am lonely for the rains
of that dirty city, for the ruins that cried with me
until the streets shone and then my face shone,
when I learned who would still toss me

the coins of kindness the way I gave change
to beggars who made me drunk on the wine
of stories. I am lonely for their eyes
that took me in, thirsty for what the dark
nights do, the surprise bird chirp an hour
before dawn. I miss such tattered songs.

# Give Me a Lover

Give me a lover who wears flannel
like the mountain boys before the Age
of Metrosexuals, a retro-heterosexual
who knows how to make things
with his hands, handsomely animal,
sweat dripping until he shines.

Give me a lover with a body
like a funky halo, skin I can
kiss and lick until my tongue
glows with the taste of salt
bearing me back to the untamed
sea, O the sweetness of he

who can rock me into waves
of ecstasy. Give me a country man
who will build me a cabin
encircled by woods starred
with the eyes of lynx and deer,
where it is okay to stay silent.

Give me a lover who wears flannel
soft enough to rest a scarred
cheek upon, one who doesn't care
about my Chanel No. 5 and fear
I might smell or taste bad
in the uptowns of good taste.

Give me a lover who can chop logs,
build a fire in a wood-stove for us,
seed me in Strawberry Moon nights
soon to blaze with fireflies
and mountain laurel. Give me
a lifetime that tastes of flannel.

# After Seeing a Facebook Picture of Chief Raoni

## Weeping Over Brazil's President Approving
## the Belo Dam Project on Xingu Land

I was thinking about Chief Raoni
yesterday when I drove back
from the Big Apple to my
beloved Catskills ...
about what so-called "progress"
means to those who love their part
of Mother Earth in a way the rootless
don't ever understand.

Of course, I don't own
the land ... no one owns it, really ...
only more and more of mountains
bleed bright orange-red posters
on trees ... so I can't wander
parts of that country anymore
 unless I sneak onto it and don't
 get caught. Maybe there are
 those of you who remember
 how it was when you could
 wander freely and dance
on Earth and not worry
about barbed wire fences,
electric fences, and the bleeds
of posters warning KEEP OFF.

I spotted two deer near old apple trees
along Elm Hollow Road … one
a yearling doe, one a spike horn.
I stopped my red pearl Subaru,
rolled down window
and lowly spoke to doe and buck …
watching ears flick back
and forth, wondering if they need
fear me who appears like the pale
shadows who strung the fences …
smiling at those deer trespassing
on posted land … their silence, my
soft voice … my silence when
they leaped into the rain music
of September woods.

I took photographs of
Elm Hollow Road and old road
along Beaverkill River … in rain,
in mists … land I call
heart country … land
where my heart song began.
One of my biggest fears?
That anyone would ever blast
off tops of Catskill Mountains
as men have done in West Virginia,
Illinois … to me
unbearable.

What if the future has
nothing left of the mountaintops
except photographs such as mine?

What if the future mechanically
combs the twigs and leaves
out of wind-braided hair?
What if she has no more
 two-leggeds like me ... no
 wisdom-haired elders old enough
to remember rambling freely
among elms, the turning
 leaves and un-fenced
woodlands, lakes and creeks?
What if the birds ...
the other two leggeds ...
cease singing because there flame
no more trees?

What if the future loses her memory?
What if she even forgets
how to weep the way
Chief Raoni cried over
 his people's rain forest lost forever
to the "progress" of fencing
in freedom and flooding all
the Beauty Ways?

# The Butterfly Funeral (for Vernon Turner)

Fall sunset at blackberry patch horizon,
wild rose skyline, quarter moon rising ...
friends a constellation encircling Fox Mountain fire.

In among the drinking and laughter someone
must have mentioned God, or said there is no God,
because Vernon starts marveling about a monarch butterfly

dead on leafy ground ... the morning he saw
monarchs dazzle down to the one who had died,
dancing black-webbed wings back and forth.

*Can you explain something like that, huh?*
*Monarchs surrounding a dead butterfly then*
*swirling up til sun sparked their wings to stained glass?*

I wonder if Vernon is going to smile or cry ...
*How do you tell people you saw a butterfly funeral?*
Some blink when wind blows smoke our way,

I blink remembering Vernon in times gone by,
homegrown wild boy defying soul death. Back then
we were all monarchs, skins coppery with summer,

bodies flaming through milkweed to skinny-
dip in butterfly shimmers of Catskill rivers.
My sister used to call Vernon *Adonis* before

milkweed and monarchs grew less each year.
In firelight his eyes glow blue-green as though
Heaven and Earth had come together again.

*How do you explain butterflies appearing*
*to feel the same as you and I?* He lilts to us
with hair metamorphosed to milkweed silk ...

we old friends a cocoon around mountain fire,
autumn arms in flannel brushing other arms
back into wings.

# Happy Indians (for Evan T. Pritchard)

No, friend, I don't care to review
other Natives' work about Rez Indians,
urban Indians, or any other Indians doing
too many drugs, drinking too much,
or beating and raping their familiars
they claim to love. Sweet brother,
you know my poetry doesn't play
to the pretty, but I need a vacation
from genocide and being colonized ...
even if an American one of just two weeks.

I yearn to rove far from intertribal warfare
sparked by who has a CDIB card and who
stays card-free and visionary as Crazy Horse ...
distant from Nations who own casinos
while the old time Indians disdain
keeping up with the Trumps.
My brother, let us go on a road trip
to a village called Joy, let's fly
down a resurrected Route 66,
leaving behind our tears for the jackpot

of driving a 1960s' pony convertible,
warm spring wind kissing our smiles.
Let us shake loose our long hair forever,
toss away ties to that world demanding
we dress in a way that imprisons
our skins born for freedom rides.

Who told us we can't be happy?
Who decreed we must keep picking
the scabs of our tragic history, make
a speech about it every chance we get?

Friend, I wax rapturous just dreaming
about our trip. May you wear your
blue ribbon shirt that transforms you
into sky. I shall wear a shawl
earth-green. And when we stop
in Joy to eat strawberries by a singing
river, I pray you play your flute
in harmony with its weaving songs.
*By the sunlit water, the star–like sparkles ...*
*we Indians, we happy Indians.*

# Whoever You Are

I invite you to where I live in Catskills,
this house I don't own but dwell in like a cat …
a poet cat. I imagine you might smile
at the many colors the interior is painted in,
rooms reflecting the multitudes I contain,
my spirit landscape mirroring mountains,
valleys, rivers, lakes, and sky shape-
shifting from day to night, season
to season. Sisters and brothers in poetry,
story weavers, flowering word warriors,
I would love for you to visit me …
eat breakfast pancakes that rhyme,
drizzled with maple syrup and hyperboles
of scarlet strawberries. We could foresee
the mystery journey before you,
together bead words no longer in fashion …
purity, bravery, integrity, simplicity.
I shall make sure it is spring, fragrant
with apple blossoms. We can palaver
outside near the ancient spruces,
maybe for dessert behold a bald eagle
spiraling above the breeze-blown
trees fancy dancing the way we prefer
to merge our own limbs with a wilder
air. I promise to listen to your stories,
honor your visions, dispel any fears
you may have concealed behind
some fake toughness. And you

might lift your faces up to May sun,
let rays like white violets heal
violent wounds. I yearn to bring you
to where I first created, to say
"See that small town beginning
at street's end? That town attempted
to make me small as itself, its gossips
and rednecks tried to mock the poetry
out of me. I wrote on in shy solitude,
cried a loneliness they would never see."
For sixty five years I have carried
my mountain Indian words in a bundle,
my medicine, my own Beauty Way.
Please come by. We'll drink some
homemade blueberry wine. You can
taste how poetry keeps us from vanishing.

# On Autumn Equinox I Wake

in Adirondacks to slow cold rain
whose drops shimmy across cabin
windows, a dance burst down
from Sky. My man left to feed
the Samoyeds about an hour ago ...
not quite sure, for I still half roam
in the country of dream that has
no time. Even some names slip by ...
through one window I see
nameless lake laced by mist,
and my seeing is of a babe
who has learned no other language
but cry and smile. Invisible
through the windblown dawn
loon calls flutter low as lullabies,
long haunting trills migrating
up off mountain water
rain has stirred into countless
cats' paws. Far away ...
cities and the busy people
who haven't forgotten how
to be important. Here
on this far north peninsula
shape-shifting to a coat
of many colors ...
just a loony poet and old man
taking care of smiling dogs
with fur thick as snow
soon to come.


(for John Gunther)

# Just Jim (for Jim Curtis)

Jim was an old friend of John's, my mate
aka Raised-by-Wolves. Long Night Moon …
Jim's first visit to the house John bought
in Catskills, place I dwell in like a feral cat
never sure if she will stay or leave to prowl
with lynxes whose eyes glow in our mountains
deepest in. Jim swirled through front door
like a wind trying to elude winter's inevitable
snows, shedding his boots and coat. Soon
we were warming the kitchen with talk
and body heat, along with the meat on the stove.
And somehow the matter of my being "part
Indian" arose, then Jim's eyes shone like those
of the wild felines who haunt these forests,
fingers tearing off shirt to show his tattoo
on a summit of biceps …Thunderbird
bringing Sky and Earth together in the cave
of our kitchen. I said, "I figured you were
Indian." "Ojibwa," he grinned

We began talking about Indian ways
and how much had been lost during
the genocide that still hadn't stopped
enough, all you had to do was look at
our suicide rates and the children still crying
and the ones who had died at their own hands.
I mentioned we always regarded gay people
as having medicine, calling them Two-Spirits.

"Oh," Jim said, "so did John tell you about me?"
I had to confess, "Yes. I just wanted you
to know you have in me a sister and friend."
"I appreciate that, but what I really want to be
is just Jim," Jim said. "You know what I mean?
Not gay, not Indian, not from Michigan, not a man
who rides a motorcycle. Just Jim minus assumptions."

"I know," I sighed, while Raised-by-Wolves
carried the meat to table shining under dining room
light, and I brought the salad, squash and red wine.
"It's like that Zen reference to the face you had
before you were born, but we all journey so far
from *that* once people hurt us into masks."
Truth is, I dug that Jim was an Indian Two-Spirit
who rode a Triumph Tiger in the starry nights,
Thunderbird shielded by black leather coat.
And I thought if someday life grew just
we could celebrate freely who we are,
become sacred once more. That night I found
a brother in among our chatter and laughter …
that winter moon we three friends decided
to rove in the Scottish Highlands
come spring.

# Letting Herself Go

*(A whistling woman is up to no good)*

*Awful, she's letting herself go*
town gossips hissed
whenever a woman they
assumed was like them
suddenly appeared with that
suspect appearance of no
longer caring if she combed
her hair or masked her face
with scar-concealing make-up
or cooked and cleaned
and tended to everyone else
while inside
bit by bit she died
behind "make nice" smiles
unless she chose to
let herself go
take back the starry night
light of her soul.

Whenever you glimpsed
the women who had *gone*
you wondered why the gossips
bemoaned such windswept hair,
easy sensuous loping bodies,
the dropped abusive husbands
and resurrections of

laughter, poetry and song
nearly forgotten. Although
merely a mountain girl
sun-fired and freckling
through the infinite summers
of playing hide-and-go-seek
in firefly nights flashing
mystery green-gold,
you soon learned the game
of hiding your dream
to grow into a woman
who lets herself go.

At seventeen you went
away from the gossips
in their girdled non-lives,
and you let your brassieres go
(ahhhh, the first to go),
you let your permanents go,
you let your high heels go,
you let your lipsticks go,
you let yourself go
for three university degrees
before dancing out
into the universe,
a full-time poet
*singing yourself* the way
the men had no problem
with playing Walt Whitman,
whistling your way cross-country
then around the world.

*Awful, she's letting herself go*
you occasionally hear the sneers
as you blaze on by, so full of awe
you let it go and pray your sisters
will wake one wild rose dawn
sane enough to let themselves go
in your joyful tracks to Iceland's
tundra of horses shaggy maned
as you, to Scotland's Highlands
and north to Orkneys where Selkies
let their seal skins go, to Queen Maeve's
cairn in Ireland, Wales' Snowdonia,
and all great cities of rovers and lovers,
Dublin, Paris, Amsterdam, Rome
and many dazzling others, and, oh,
how you let yourself go.

# PART II

"All journeys have secret destinations of which the traveler is unaware."

Martin Buber

# Before Language, Reutigen, Switzerland (for Beat Stähli)

Before language, it must have been like Reutigen
where my man and I once babysat a Shanghai cat
whose orange feline meows singed the air
like extravagant voices in Chinese opera ...
where we couldn't understand the villagers'
Swiss German, Alpine dialect drifting into
my ears softly as the dialect where I come from
in New York Catskills, the snow music of it.

Before language, it must have been like this,
no names for countries, mountains, plants and beasts ...
long time ago when ancestors and ancestresses
spoke in the Ur language of smiles, lights in eyes,
body dances and hands flying birdlike through air.
Back then we must have petted each other
like sleek cats ... when we hadn't forgotten
to bow to the mystery of us.

Before language, it is said that men and women
walked equal as they did in Orkney Islands'
Skara Brae, Neolithic village near sea whose tide
washed Selkies onto shore. Before words, seals
shed their skins, made love with humans,
created descendants like me with webbed toes.
Magical, free, no one doubted we could shape-shift
and communicate with hearts of beauty.

Before language, no one argued about religion
or believed anyone was better than anybody else.
Ask Beat Stähli, woodcarver relative who dwells
in my Swiss great grandmother's Heimat of Brienz.
O my brother, my cousin, my friend, still I see you
dreaming through atelier window across ancient lake ...
still there be knowing Souls not separate
from water spirits and the holy trees.

# Parka (for Jon Sveinsson)

That April night past Reykjavik,
along Atlantic, Jon swung open
door to Iceland's spring
winds carrying Viking voices
and whistlings of ancient skáld
seeking some shelter for sleeping
before sleet or even snow cried in
with all hints of summer lost.
At first you thought your friend
was stepping out to smoke his pipe,
and in your warm nook you mused
how nothing seemed to disappear
on that island of ice and fire.
And was it any wonder its elves
and trolls still lived? Wonder

as it turned out was what Jon
sought, and seeing it
he called your mate and you …
*Come, come, the Northern Lights*
*are shying across the sky.*
Dearest Jon, fulfilling your dream
of meeting the lights that dance
before you died. He offered
to drive you up near the lighthouse
where Reykjavik's neon
blazed less. Yes, it blew
ghostly cold and he gave you

his parka to wear for sighting
whatever that night might bring
when you rode further on

by black sea crashing against
gnome-like stones. How old
you had grown, and Jon dubbed
himself "old man" despite being
the youngest there. Only
your mate could joke he was really
just sweet sixteen. Flotsam of a
different crashing, you and Jon
were too poor to afford illusions.
Iceland lived up to its name that eve
of leaving, yet Aurora Borealis
made half the sky emerald,
the mirror half gilded by moonrise,
while inside Jon's great parka
your scars shimmered into stars.

# Icelandic Horse Dreaming

Back home in America
I remember you the way
I recall dreams, yet even
when a girl dreaming
of stallions I never
imagined flying to Iceland
with a future love or staying
with a Reykjavik friend
who would drive us to see
Hestur, Icelandic Horse,
not far from hot springs
whose steam whirled up from
hesitant April Earth like herds
of spirit horses mating with
the unsaddled winds.

Back on Turtle Island
I cradle photographs
of awakening brown field
beyond the roadside fence,
where pony-like horses
of many shaggy colors
pranced to each other,
rearing up in frisky forecasts
of midnight suns and whatever
means love in the land of pure
and ancient horses. We three,
Jon and John and me, tugged free
old grasses and offered tufts
of "the other side of the fence"
to horses tölting softly to us,

and she who came to me
had a blaze like Big Bang
starlight down her nose,
nuzzling my blue wool sweater.
In the pictures Jon wears
traditional Icelandic sweater,
John a grey fleece, and to my eyes
they appear horse shaggy
and just as gentle.
I loved them all in that land
where Earth's fierce heart
swells so near its skin of moss,
lichens and volcanic stone,
ice married to fire. Forever
our trinity remains frozen

in images of heads bowed
to you, Hestur of beach
browns and ember reds, ice
whites and volcano blacks.
When I tölt through
the steams of that seeming
dream, fly back over
invisible night sea into
an Iceland of turquoise sky,
it is as if I am First Poet
with hands flamed open
to such rough maned
but sweet mannered Horse
nuzzling the fate lines,
beginning the sagas.

# Medhbh

It be May in Ireland, you
and your lover seeking
Queen Maeve's cairn atop
Knocknarea ... that poet warrior
whose hair sparked down
her eight feet length til it
touched quartz white feet,
until there, there, you spot
Maeve's cairn like a bold nipple
even in fog, as if King Ailill

had just kissed it. Your mate
drives you through gorse yellow
as joy, coconut scents adrift
in strands of mist evoking
ancient spirits and fairies silvery.
Then trail head sign ...
"Great stone mound was probably
erected circa 2500 B.C." Ambling
up pebbly path you feed grass
to auburn mares, recall

how the flame-haired queen
outran stallions and caused
enemy soldiers to lie down
in awe when they beheld
her thighs and lyrical mouth,
Medhbh meaning intoxicating.

It be May in County Sligo,
rain gleaming like swords
of a mythic time. Tis
a bit of a hike, and near

breathless you feel when you
pass the rise that lets old eyes
behold Queen Maeve's cairn
close up. Be it true she stands
inside that hive of rocks,
upright with her warrior's shield?
O you can only kneel
where it brings good fortune
to leave a stone, bad luck
to steal one off the cairn ...

give vala airy as gull bone,
volcanic stone from an epic
Icelandic friend, honor Medhbh's
fire waiting inside the ash
of centuries. And who passes
as your king kneels by you
who once had fiery hair. Two
violets glisten near the mound,
Ailill and Maeve, he and I,
and rhyming down ... the rain.

# Poeteen (for Frank & Margaret)

That morning in Muckross her man
drove them from the B & B not far
from sea caves they explored
the night before during lingering May
sunset, following village road
more like dirt path until after
a swooping turn they beheld
a cove sun-laved and sparkling
as though Ireland had forgotten
her mists. Such a calm shelter
within the rebel ocean off
County Donegal, luring them
to wade and swim and pick up
shiny stones and shells
for when they were back
in America's Catskills whose
great sea was lost eons ago.

She called this one of her homelands,
she with Irish ancestress and feeling
ancient connection to the shamrock isle.
They played in the waters like two seals,
felt metamorphosed into man and woman
when they climbed back up the
low cliff where they met Frank
who turned out to be ninety-one,
a fisherman until three years ago.
They talked back and forth

like the sparkles leaping
across the waves, and when
Frank learned she was a poet
he invited them into his house
to drink poteen with Himself
and Margaret his wife
like him old but young.

O that poteen he poured them,
halfway up the little glasses, clear
as spring water where the fairies
commune by the holy wells.
She sipped the Muckross moonshine
distilled above peat the people
in County Donegal still cut and dug up
for warmth of many kinds.
Frank and Margaret said
it was made of barley when she
marveled over the hint of taste
her tongue could not quite define,
maybe petrol about to glint
into flame. Her mate kept joking
about her seeking the fairies
whenever they stopped at
"those stone circles." Fierce
she pouted, "We didn't see them
because of your mockery.
Fairies won't approach anyone
who doubts they exist."

Her very first poteen tasting
of the fires of poetry,
of the first time she ever wrote ...
and at first she imagined
Frank's and Margaret's smiles
and eyes twinkling as much
as the cove that day
had to do with her fairy story.
But then she started sliding
off Earth's mothering curve,
felt shoulder blades
sprouting wings,
so she put down gently
her little glass and chirped
through lips becoming beak,
"I really appreciate the poteen
you gave me, but if I drink
one more drop I shall see
a hundred fairies dancing!"

Only Herself tweeted "poeteen"
and the dapper fisherman
and his dancing darling
of over seventy years
laughed and laughed.

# The Fairy of County Donegal

There was the dancer lilting to us as after we picked her up hitchhiking
on a drunk cliff road high above County Donegal sea edge, we three moving
through Irish May of yellow gorse and rose-and-white rhododendron flamed
forth in spring sun. She in back seat, me hoping we would put her at ease
because well I know how a woman hitchhiker never is sure about being safe
when she clambers into a stranger's car. If ever I saw an Irish fairy it was she
in diaphanous dress, coral and lavender dream hugged by green wool shawl,
hair glittering silver-blond down lithe back past buttocks, thighs, hilly rises,
and eyes so emerald they glowed like gems some wizard embedded in skin
where human eyes should have been. But, fairy-like, she did not appear
concerned we might harm Herself smiling fearless at us, we three a trinity
riffing off the blaze of each others' words in that way talk goes with winged
ones in motion. Alighting on the matter of travelers and Gypsies, she said
the travelers were the original Irish of that isle anointed by the coconut scent
of gorse gracing goldly the ancient coast still in love with the wild crone sea.
Not the same, she tossed her head, as the Gypsies driven from India, vowing
they'd wander from land to land until that elusive hour when they can at last
return. Next her musing question sprinkling eternal fairy dust across my
Gypsy soul, Why is it normal for us to remain in a single spot? Why is
domesticity the better way to be? Why isn't the natural state roaming
free from place to place, with all of mothering Earth one's embracing home?
We left the dancer in the village she was hitchhiking to, waving our hands
like re-found wands, Oh, farewell, farewell! How few people still can smile
that way the dancer smiled, all laughing heart, first roving starlight
of her fairy self not lashed down to owning or being owned.

# Webbed Toes (for John Corney)

Brother remembering Grandfather's
webs so high up toes his feet
looked like frog's feet, how Grandpa
would show him the webs then laugh.
Webs strong-delicate. Webs evoking
Orkney Isles Selkies, sea creatures
who hide skins on beach
then mate with humans.

The Scotch-Irish sailed here,
mixed their Orkney DNA
with Turtle Island Native blood.
When my brother and I lift our feet
light glows through seal skin,
reminding me of sun rays
shimmering through
pale blue rice in China bowls,

of all the lights I have met with
lovely as any that have flown
into my eyes. Webs threading back
to Mongolia, to Orkney Isles,
to seas of mystery. And there comes
some powerful gentleness I bring
to land whenever I press foot soles

to Mother Earth, leaving
slow trail of ancient light
that makes my clan be as children
forever slipping off shoes, boots,
sandals, moccasins, raising up
freedom feet to delight in their webs
and the metaphor of toes, old
knowing of wild north seas
and kisses of Selkies.

# The Seals of the River Ythan

Early May morning north of Aberdeen ...
John, our friend, Jim, and me following
the River Ythan to where the seals
were mating. For Scotland, a sunny day ...
sky blue as the eyes of clansmen in black leather
on motorcycles we met along the way,
clouds like Highlands crowned with snow.
John and Jim strode far ahead ...
I, old devotee of dawdling, kneeling
to touch wet pebbles and broken shells.
Black-and-white Mergansers quacked
duck passion across the silvery stream in long
intercourse with windswept shore edged by gorse,
coconut scent mingling with North Sea smells
of rotting seaweeds and dead fish not yet picked
clean by gulls. Then the men disappeared.
Having liberated my old brown hiking shoes,
barefoot I ran to where they had strolled
into the sun, becoming twin glimmers barely
human flesh at all. They, also, had kicked off
shoes, each claiming a spot from where to watch
countless seals in the starry Ythan and on its opposite
shore. Wordless I found my own watching place,
in my silence praying the seals would swim near.
I am your relative, my azure awe sought to say.
I have webbed toes, and you know we women
of the webs descend from Selkies who shed
their seal skins and had to marry men

who stole those skins so they could not take
their sleek beauty back to the bereft sea.
And hard it was for John, our friend, Jim, and me
to keep from laughing with rapture pure as blue ...
when the seals' songs licked our ears with notes
such as we had not ever heard, boundless brogues
in chant-like crescendos kissing the salty air.
Curious, the seals swam close, diving into
waves then popping up like periscopes,
glossy lovelorn eyes surveying us to see
if we'd make sweet mates. How to sing
my Isle blood still remembered
such seal desire ... and the blue-eyed love
of the clansman who took my skin?

# Clootie Well (for Anne Ryan)

And long I yearned to visit one of those wells
renown for healing centuries before Christians
and patriarchy ruled in that Isle now broken
into Scotland, Ireland, England, Wales ...

until at last in this gorse-scented May
I roam back to where many of my
ancestresses dwelled and wandered
barefoot on springy moss, old evergreen

needles, roots, and stepping stones ...
make my pilgrimage to Clootie Well,
Munlochy, Scotland, encircling trees
draped with rags, cloths, clothes,

some new, others rotting,
the rest deteriorated beyond all
color and recognition. Spill
three drops of water on earth, tie

a rag around a tree trunk or branch,
drink from the well, make a wish
and you will have good luck ...
belief the folk still follow,

although my roving companion
smirks this must be Cootie Well
when I hesitate to drink the water
squeezing out through a bank

below a hanging garden of ghosts
wrapped in rot their last hope.
And don't others say what hurts
will heal if you cleanse your pain

with water-dipped cloth, leave it
to rot ... that moment the cloth
becomes wild air your wound flies
away and you are as a bird again?

My mother and her mother told
about our red-haired ancestresses
who sang and flamed in wooded places
leafing out in May, their eyes
that same green plush
with reborn light. In America
I heard them calling, calling,
across the sea and centuries,

singing me back to when we
went roving with goddesses and knew
how to heal and be free and lucky,
barefoot women of the sacred wells.

# The Hooved Daughter of Dornoch's Last Witch

If only those hypocrites who claimed
they adored Christ hadna taken over Scotland
and her auld wild ways when we still
carried The Highlands and Selkie seas
within our unbowed hearts, could fly
back and forth between this life
and other realms where we danced free.
Them with their fake souls never
conceded Jesus was one who flew
into such Spirit Worlds and spoke a poetry
called parables. Nae, they chained love
inside the dungeon of judgment,

so when they decreed my aging mother ...
and myself with deformed hands and feet ...
were witches, I yearned in my trembling
for our land before she was raped and ruled
by such as Sheriff Ross who ordered
we be stripped, tarred, and burned
the following morn. Mother could
only *greet* in her once melodious tongue ...
*I've tried to live a good life, but my people*
*are strangers to me now. My girl has*
*a twisted hand and they whisper terrible*
*things about us. Why do they hate us so?*

Ay, why did those church-going gossips
imagine my maw had turned me into
a pony she could ride to lay with their Devil …
or up to azure sky past the *dreich*
of icy drizzle, she and I laughing
in sunshine beyond their gloom.
Shrieking, they didn't hear Mother's
whisper to me, "Escape, my darlin',
fly far away before they murder you
with me tomorrow." And I flew,
no one knew how, and now there be
what they call "The Witch's Stone"
marking where the mob burned

my mother after they tarred
and feathered and dragged her naked
in a barrel over their stony streets.
Yet she smiled when they
torched the tar to flames …
*Oh, what a bonny blaze!*
Some believe she was senile,
but I say Mother always loved beauty,
lived brave, and facing death
made a stand for that heart's fire
the braying mob had not the heart
to understand. By then I was hiding
further north by Dornoch's Firth,
witch daughter with the *twisted hand*
weeping salt tears into the salty sea,

for I still saw Mother with her red hair
carrying me there in her arms
when it hurt to walk, soothing me
with stories of girls who could
shape-shift into bright ponies and fly
without pain at every step, she lilting
*Lassie, what a bonny blaze ye be.*
Oh, Mither, dear Mither, I vowed
that day of wading barefoot to soothe
the remnants of my hooves,
our bards would sing you as more
than a forsaken stone pockmarked
with lichens.

# Gypsy Caravan, April 1985

April I lived with the old professor
teaching in London for one semester,

sojourned on a demure street that dipped
like a curtsy near Hampstead Heath

not far from Keats' house and the knoll
where Gypsies parked a wooden caravan

carved in flowers painted primary hues
of daffodils, tulips, grass emerald green.

April my sister called from Catskills,
"The doctors say Mom's breast cancer

is terminal." We cried, I choked I'd fly home,
but our mother's voice bloomed into the phone,

"No, stay in England. You always wished
to travel. I won't die right away." Spring day

I traipsed with husband across the Heath,
tried to shake off grief, asked him

for five pounds when I lingered
near the great golden halo of a palm

promising one's fortune could be told
inside the caravan of eye-like flowers.

He clenched hands into fists, spat
it was all Gypsy lies ... reading heart

and destiny lines. We had one of those
fights, he stomped off in tweed jacket

he thought made him into D.H. Lawrence,
pretentious patches on elbows punching air

still sweet despite our human affairs. I stood
with empty hands like drooping snowdrops

pressed to trailing skirt blue as sky ...
desiring good fortune, a lifeline.

# Gypsy of Lausanne

Gypsy of Lausanne, I did not realize
you were begging when I spotted you
on stone bench near door to the Cathedral
Notre Dame that my man and I had no
intention of entering after tromping
up there from Avenue Bergières where we
amazed ourselves at the Collection de l'Art Brut,
communing with the raw free beauty of the mad ...
and I, the poet, thinking there but for the grace
of the goddess go I and maybe that wouldn't be
so bad. We were only breathless for the sake
of the view, yearning to look out across winter's
religion of roofs and bare trees black notes
in that Saturday's adagio of raindrops,

until we found the other view ... you, Gypsy,
poised smiling like a bird of paradise
or flower sprung forth from another universe
where it is always summer and people
greet passersby because there it is
impossible to be a stranger. Yes, I took
root in the same universe you flamed from,
smiling, too, until we were flashing
back and forth like a sisterhood of shooting
stars, and I swear I slipped out of man-made
time into the holy past where my ancestresses
dressed like you in your red poppy kerchief
and long checked skirt dotted with pink buds.

Gypsy woman of Lausanne, I did not see
the small begging bowl by your side,
but my man whispered to me about the bowl
so I glided closer and dropped in
euros like raindrops, hoped it was okay
to ask you to pose for a couple of photos
side by side, s'il vous plait. You rose up
and our smiles bloomed into laughter,
we with hair hue of rain headed for snow ...
holding each other girlish against glacial winds
hallucinating down from Alps. Merci,
for I did not want to forget again the universe
where people grow faces wise as yours, Gypsy,
where it is always summer and no one's a stranger.

# That Winter in Torremolinos

That winter in Torremolinos the dark grief
of your mother's death two moons ago
remained the deep song moaning through
your veins, and even Andalusian sun
could not shine away the shadow
in your marrow unable to forget the cancer
that ate her bones until even her neck
broke. Your old professor husband
had wanted to fly away from New York
snows, while you no longer cared
where your sorrow flew. And so
one morning your feet led you
out of shuttered rooms down

the oldest streets of Torremolinos,
gaiety of houses flamed with hues
equaling a rainbow, wandering until
you glimpsed the Mediterranean
beyond a Cubism of rundown huts,
stucco crumbling off walls.
A dog imprisoned inside
backyard fence barked, lunged
at you concealing a crumbled
heart. Startled you stared, hearing
your mother whisper she wished she
had lived a freer life as chemo dripped
poison into her arm, tears following
her regret now drowning your face
in a foreign land.

A Gypsy man appeared as though
he had whirled out of the bright air,
left hand holding a blue guitar,
right hand held out towards dog
wolf-immense. Fingers flamenco-like
in reach, he spoke in low voice
soothing as sea waves lapping up
to shore on a calm day, patient, tender,
as though courting someone who had
never been transported by love's "Olé!"
The yellow-eyed dog ceased barking,
bowed black head against fence where
the Gypsy stroked her uncombed hair,
then started strumming sky
of guitar. You swayed smiling,
watching him dispel pain and rage,
that magical Gypsy man
in violet shirt and unbuttoned vest
flapping like two wings flying free
until he turned and smiled back
your fortune to you, your "Ole!"

*There, there, Love, you will be okay.*

## Starry Night Over the Rhone
## ... to Vincent Van Gogh

Dear Vincent, how could I have foreseen
that October day, riding subway train to MOMA,
not knowing until I arrived about the exhibit
of your night paintings? You who penned
letters to Theo, wrote your holy fire
to the most beautiful brother who ever lived ...

*The terrible ordeals of suffering are what teach you*
*to look at things with different eyes.*

How elated I felt even while waiting
two red-leafed hours in line a long brushstroke ...
but these eyes are just different enough that for you
I would have swayed for eternity in anticipation.

At last the ticket-taker in uniform purple
like a bruise waved me through door.
As though my smile broke the sound barrier
of any possible words for entering into

that entrancement of paintings
and Nature which you loved so much,
in my awe I heard yellow, your favorite color
and mine, my body flaming around mid-room wall
to surprise of "Starry Night Over the Rhone,"
no human mind left in me to impose on

aquamarine sky, Great Bear furred
with sparkling stars, river you painted
royal blue, Arles quay mauve below gas lights
brutal gold to your eyes maddening with
modern times tearing in as my eyes teared
with such deep, thick spiraling, the Great Bare
of my atoms recalling another letter …

*Any woman, at any age, if she loves*
*and is a good woman, can give a man not*
*the infinity of a moment, but a moment of infinity.*

Beloved Vincent, would you paint me
as good, this poor poet halting in the jostle
of art lovers, intelligentsia, and high society poseurs
ignorant of any terrible ordeals except to "get off"
on the alchemies of your suffering, my suffering,
nearly falling to my wounded knees
that have tried not to scrape across the smashed
love, tenderness, dreams the philistines
never seem to get their glut of …

"Starry Night Over the Rhone" seducing me
into its spinning heat as if into your very arms,
a sheltering upon our Mother Earth
torn open for greed's fool's gold?

Vincent, I nearly knelt down
in torn stockings black as crows
hugging my legs, enraptured
enough to embrace your colors,
starry Big Bang of sky, mirror
of female water,

poised to give your painting
real head, to swallow your stars
in front of all those superior people.

# Beggar, St. Peter's Square

This beggar woman could be another Gypsy …
hard to tell on vast square prelude
to Vatican City, among tourist shops
glutted with Madonnas and Baby Jesuses
made in China. Some Europeans warn
"Love your neighbor as yourself"
does not apply to the Roma, those rovers
viewed as nobody's neighbors, existing here,
there and everywhere to pick the pockets
of the respectable. Only I wear long skirts
like the Gypsy women and have no pockets.

Beyond the Tiber and Vatican Dome
February sun descends in a long bloom
of lambent twilight unique to Rome.
The Romans delight in saying
their city's name backwards spells Amor,
and it is fierce love I feel in that purity
of azure and rose. I suppose the saintly
might find Heaven in such sky, angels
in those hints of halos. But if I see any
angel at all, she is a fallen one in the shape
of that beggar on cobblestones.

How can I, another woman, part
American Indian from centuries of outcasts,
not kneel down to where a sister is humped
across cold rock still wet from morning rains,

not feel kinship with her ankle-length skirt
grey as fog, kerchief pulled over head and face
touched to Earth also covered with grey?
How can she stay bowed all day, blind backside
exposed to tourists babbling past? My own pride
can hardly bear anything as vulnerable as that.
I find two euros in embroidered bag

I carry just for beggars and buskers,
drop them into dog bowl her hands clutch
in front of her facelessness.
The respectable scold me about being
the kind of fool they forget their Jesus was.
The beggar loosens her headscarf, reveals
young countenance and impish smile
evoking a sun rising not dying ...
and my laugh. Oh, Gypsy for sure,
like Mary Magdalene when her accusers
stopped stoning her. The other Roma,
spelled backwards ... Amor.

# Superman of the Piazza Navona

Not that she wasn't impressed when she
emerged from Via del Salvatore onto
the Piazza Navona, even in February
eyes half closing to light blazing down
on Bernini's baroque cake of a fountain,
marble giants allegories of the 17th century's
four great river ... the Nile, Danube,
Ganges and Rio de Plata. But
more than those writhing figures
she would make love to should she grow
mythic, she felt drawn to the horse
galloping through center hole as if
entering a world where no one is
made small and bereft of beauty.

Not that she didn't feel awe or extend
five fingers to caress the stallion,
almost tumbling into the starry water,
in that moment of brief pirouette
her gaze cast across the piazza
to a crowd clustering around some
unseen mystery. Never one to resist
the unseen creating a new constellation,
she caught herself and flowed in long skirt
over cobblestones to that cluster
of happiness, laughter of children
and adults, too, in the warming air.
Edging close she beheld the source
and sorcery of such delight ...

Superman with the two longest wands
for making bubbles she had ever seen
in her more than six decades
on wondrous earth, young man
choreographing a slow motion
ballet of bubbles, revolving
inside myriad transparent skins
and transient rainbows. Children
skipped around him, raising arms
to embrace big bubbles as they floated
free then rose towards Ligurian blue sky.
Sometimes one broke with a pop
like a champagne cork revealing
the sparkling joy of revels ahead,

while that boy-man in red-gold suit
smiled until her own face burst
into smiles that bubbled over
into the piazza's collective laughter ...
where the world's dissension
and despair dissipated, everyone's
arms lifted to those liberated spheres
reflecting Roma's magic light
as if they would never end
but touch whatever heaven there be.
More than all the city's churches,
the Superman of the Piazza Navona
lit her with prayer, making her
miraculous with his dance of hands.

# Today I Jaywalked in Leipzig

Today I jaywalked in Leipzig, even though
my mate joked before we flew to Germany
that Germans don't even jaywalk at 3 a.m.
when the streets yawn empty and it seems
no one can see. His father ein Berliner,
he is in the "know" about waiting
for pre-dawn green lights. Today I broke

the law, despite all the good Germans waiting,
nary a car in sight, most of them with bikes.
And I am not sure what made me go, go, go
on the red, perhaps summer solstice nearly here,
or the Stasi Museum where we learned more
about the Secret Police and fear, or because
I am ein New Yorker und ein Mohawk,

and, Liebchen, in New York it's WALK
when no cars are coming, RUN
when they are, and if someone curses you
or toots their horn, shoot them the bird.
Today I jaywalked in Leipzig, glancing back
at my mate where he paused then tore
loose from the crowd, worthy of a "boy

from Brooklyn," laughing as we left
the bicyclists with their slim trim bodies
behind on the curb. Und I recalled
the German I fell in love with in Berlin's

Topography of Terror Museum,
one unsmiling man in 1930s
black-and-white photo, arms folded

over chest while a herd of Germans
surrounding him raised their arms
in "Heil, Hitler" shrieks. I hoped
the man still lived, wished to kiss him
as if I were an untouched girl again
and he untouched by the SS
who arrested those refusing to whip

the air with an arm and idiot shout.
I bowed to that hero's heart beneath
its cross of arms, its passion
defying the crowd. Und I prayed
that all the gut Americans won't cave
in to fascists and hate. Ja, today in Leipzig
my lover and I jaywalked to an ode of joy.

# Hiroshima Schoolboy: Tankas in Four Parts

on the Anniversary of the Bombing of Hiroshima

### I.

It shone like a bird.
My best friend danced out to it.
I watched by a wall.
My friend waved at the strange wings.
He laughed as the dark egg fell.

### II.

I turned blind at first.
If only I had stayed blind.
Friend shadow on stone
after the egg cracked open.
Pretty chrysanthemum cloud.

### III.

In time the funerals.
We lost all words, even hell.
I became a wall.
The mothers wouldn't look at me.
Why didn't I die, their sons live?

IV.

A bright bird he was.
His raven's hair shone unruly.
He'd be a poet.
Oh, friend, nothing touches me.
Except I bow to your fire.

# Chinese Boxes

The woman on the outer box
carved in nephrite,
dark green, exquisite,
but hard to the touch ...

a regular museum piece, her husband allows,
impossible to break in her jade gown.

At night, this same woman laid down
in gold leaf on the polished second box,
divided in three like an old screen,
listens as her husband's hands
claw at stone.

On the next box black calligraphy,
the woman an ancient poem at dawn,
brush strokes racing like whipped horses
across lacquered wood.

In a fourth box, inside rough planks,
the woman collects things in the rain ...
spider webs, green beetles, broken glass.

In the smallest box, squeezed
to the size of a small girl,
barefooted, twigs in her hair
the woman talks to her imaginary self,

as her husband displays to all his friends
the perfect jade carving
on the first box.

# Yellow Umbrellas

Winter nights she dreams of the umbrellas
blossoming in young people's hands, thousands
of blossoms for shelter from Hong Kong sun
and police attacks with water cannons
and pepper spray. She dreams of umbrellas yellow
as daffodils that will return with spring, no longer
underground, liberated by soft light. During
nor'easters she nestles old face and snow hair
into her cat's fur, dreaming she is nineteen,
protesting war and other injustices on D.C. streets.
So many faces opening like umbrellas.
So many umbrellas trembling like wildflowers.
Past lovers wave peace signs to her and sing
"We shall overcome." The student who defied
the tank years ago in Tiananmen Square
runs smiling to her and kisses her with lips
that feel like petals. Oh, you are alive?
She kisses him back. The visionaries
of the Occupy Movement camp in her dreams.
She brings them water and sleeping bags again.
On Hunger Moon nights people raise up
umbrellas all around Mother Earth, yellow
umbrellas of freedom, an orange cat,
the weeping stars of her sleep.

# After Reading Sam Hamill's
## *Crossing the Yellow River*

in bathtub, she floats to sleep thinking about
Tu Fu, Li Po, and other ancient Chinese poets,

dreams she dwells on mountainside
with those two poet pals who give her rice

they bummed from the mountain monastery,
even sharing their wine with the young

green-eyed woman in her dream. She can't
decide which bad boy she loves more,

possibly Li Po because of that way he gazes
so ridiculously at full moon glittering on lake.

Behind door she hears male voice cry
"Hellooo!" Crossing back over the river

between sleep and waking, she shines
"I'm here, Li Po. Come in!" But no one

comes. She gazes at old woman's body
in tub-lake size of a coffin.

# Cabin

A brother writes about moving
to his north woods' cabin,
leaving the old life behind,
with its big house, dead
marriage, rooms empty even
with fancy furniture in them.

You smile to think of him
in a cabin under northern lights
flaring like the inside of a body
when it makes love to the one
it was waiting for since birth.

You used to believe you would live
that way. Catskill Indian girl,
you thought you couldn't endure
cities for long. Only it was that *shine*
the old people noticed in you ...

*You were born to wander, it's in*
*your eyes, child, they dance away*
*from your face.* You knew then ...
your eyes two jade birds
made to fly away from those
who stayed in one place.

Yes, another wanderer, a brother,
writes about his cabin, wood stove,
the kind of fire you dreamed into
when your mother was still alive
and you could visit home ...
resting head on knapsack
by stove's glass panes red-lit.

January night, snow drifts
softer than death on city roof.
Cat curls on your thighs like smoke.

# Panda (for Manuela)

Jim and I waited in early spring air to view
baby pandas at the Toronto Zoo ...

my dream since I was a toddler
carrying a stuffed panda everywhere,

hugging the yin/yang black-and-white
of it when I slept. How happy I felt

to see real pandas for the first time
with my dear brother I had hitched

a ride with at his suggestion to visit
Midwest friends and meet Manuela

from Switzerland, a distant cousin.
Finally we wended our way to mock

bamboo forest the plump twin pandas
lived in, rolling all around, climbing,

and chewing on bamboo next to their
mother. Enough to make the staunchest

atheist believe there could be a creator ...
beholding glow-eyed creatures *so adorable*

even the world-weary forget their angst.
Nearby a sign explaining female pandas

prefer to remain alone unless they
feel a yen to mate, otherwise savoring

bamboo's green tender shoots
and the raptures of solitude.

How kindred that mother panda, drunk
as a poet on her own eccentric beauty ...

there for people to envy her
appearing to do nothing.

# Happy Man

After I cracked open the Chinese fortune cookie,
the vertical paper inside curled up joyfully
in my hand. "You are a happy man," it sang
in red letters on white. The other women
at my dining room table giggled, even though
prudes might think they were of an age beyond
giggling. I put my latest fortune on microwave top,
in that China bowl a former lover stole for me,
the one overflowing with good fortunes. Ever since
that night of my friends' giggles, *plus* raised eyebrows,
I have indeed been a happy man. I have become
a happy Chinese man, a tiny figure strolling across
ancient scroll. I even sprout white chin hairs,
so any day now I'll sport a wisp of Chinese beard.

I used to be an unhappy woman living in America …
a mixed blood Indian woman whose tears cascaded
further than her white hair. Now that I am a happy man,
I'm trying to remember why that was. Something about
living in city yet always feeling homesick for country.
Something about living in country and feeling homesick
for the past. Something about the way *everything*
seemed to have to do with money, *nothing* with family
and ceremony and vision and love. Something about
how the money-men treated women like me.

Since my fortune was made by some sun-tinged hand
in that land the 4-year-old me tried to dig holes to,
I've grown freer and freer. I smile open smiles as vast
as the valleys that stretch between those pinnacled
mountains of the beautiful scroll I travel across.
I never wear shoes. Because I am such a happy man,
my happiness doesn't feel twigs and pebbles poking
its feet. I am like those Chinese poets who lived
centuries ago, happy Chinese men like Li Po and Tu Fu,
writing poems on bark and stone, bumming rice
at the mountain monastery. I am so happy
I forget I'm wandering around like this
because I disgraced myself in the imperial city,
drinking and cloud dancing, neglecting
my official duties.

Yes, thanks to my good fortune
that my springtime fingers finally sprung
from its prison-cookie, I am a happy man.
Now I know that my real duty in life
is to write poetry, whistle, laugh, talk to wild foxes,
get drunk on stars, and sleep with deer. Now I know
my duty is to never be dutiful, only lit with love.
How sweet life is. How green these mountains.
How blue this sky that can never fire
this happy Chinese man from his happy job.

# Red Thread Vietnam Dream

We fly to South Vietnam … Teresa, A, John and I … our flying like the "beam me up, beam me down" of "Star Trek" … disintegrated into atoms here on Turtle Island, reassembled in Teresa's home country near a place of cabana type rooms. Plain and beige, the rooms have long narrow beds pushed together, torn and rumpled spreads covering mattresses sworn to secrecy. No windows, only an inner light similar to that in faces of those who flew with me. Honey bee buzz thoughts of former guests who had crossed over the rooms' thresholds … *How can we make love on those beds without their coming apart and us falling off and apart?*

We scarred lovers leave invisible suitcases on beaten floors … wander out into fierce June light but surprisingly no heat. Beyond a stretch of Day-Glo grass a river bordered by trees waving to us in a slight breeze of calligraphy … river a braiding of hues more subdued than the green tripping grass flashing like glass. Approaching river bank, we hug our bodies with bare arms as if our skin-encapsulated whirling molecules might decide to break apart … beam us up to a black hole and the next universe beyond. I fall to my knees in grass silken as the dresses of Vietnam War prostitutes in Saigon, fragrant as their long dusky hair. How many U.S. soldiers left women pregnant with daughters who would now be Teresa's age … me remembering my brother stationed on Saigon's edge, his twelve page letters, the blue haze words flaming the women in Chinatown were especially beautiful. Could there have been an infant left behind?

My face becomes a river and the sorrow of those war years war flood back, flowing down my aging body, streaming around bare feet of these three people I'm with and on down to river that does not cry but keeps singing in a bedazzlement of sun dances on its patient waters. Through the burst dam of grief my lover, John, and our younger friends shape-shift into prisms of many colors in Vietnamese air. Hues of history, shimmers of stories, poems, shredded webs of dreams … diminishing echoes of past war moratoriums in Amerika … *One, two, three, four, we don't want your fuckin' war* … so many protesters … so many young … so many dead.

*Is it okay to swim in the river?* I ask Teresa who would know if this river had alligators or the poisonous snakes of napalm and agent orange still slithering into its flowing. Teresa takes A's hand, smiles, and leads him into the water. I rise up, John and I following them in to swim in the sleepy currents. Even though the sun glows fierce, snow appears on the long reaching branches of the calligraphy of trees and my sadness cools into ice and sparkle. I swim to an upper part of the river where a Vietnamese man waits with two objects balanced on the palms of his hands … half moons with the skins of fruits, one the saffron of a Buddhist monk's robe, the other purple of Iroquois wampum. *These are our treaties for peace … here, you can touch peace now …* drawing my fingers to half moons flying together into Strawberry Full Moon. Teresa, A, John and I swim and float in moonlit waters of *Shantih Shantih Shantih*, the peace which passeth all understanding … the only snake a red thread weaving through indigo river, encircling us in waves mirroring the River of Stars … the wormholes of poetry … the invisible fiery strings binding us in love …

# French Picnics

When I studied French in high school
and sneaked off to French art films
on school nights, I used to dream
of visiting France.  Bittersweet
sixteen in 1960s, a poor girl
with little chance of going far,
I traveled in my dreams
until I escaped my small
mountain town. It helped
that I had something of Bridget
Bardot and Jeanne Moreau
about my face and limbs …
a pout, a feline slinkiness,
that made men want to be
Jean Belmondo for me,
breathless and existential.

I thought about those days
of New Wave movies ...
the love affairs worthy
of a teenage girl who thought
it an absurd mistake
she was born in America ...
when my latest lover drove us
from Alsace-Lorraine to Rheims
and Laon last June. There
in summer my daily rapture
became the picnics of red wines,

baguettes, Camembert and grapes …
transient banquets on roadside tables
or parks like the one bordering
Laon so charming on hilltop,
Persian cats languorous behind
windows framed by green shutters.

*Mon amour* chauffeured me
through butterfly vineyards lush
with grapes waxing to sweet
ripeness. How few francs
for Bordeaux and Merlot,
how ambrosial the pastries
with real cream … we drinking
in the hand-kissing sunshine.
Let us pray all children
born poor may someday go
on such journeys, abandon old
humiliations for the Heaven
of a poet's French picnics.

# Assateague Love Song

Driving back from cove and ocean
   she stops along island road,
sidles out to photograph
   Assateague ponies grazing beyond
a river's mirrored sky quieting
   towards night. Slow-motionly
she moves towards dream made true ...
   wild horses for years
she had yearned to see, equine bodies
   moving anciently,

pressing sleek to each other
   then apart into isles of shyness ...
coats pinto-spotted like puzzle
   pieces uninterested in fitting
together to form a sureness of where
   their herds originated ...
tough beauty left with
   sibilant name of Indians
murdered or run north forever
   far from sea into mountains.

Old stories speak of horses
   escaping 17th century shipwrecks,
swimming to Assateague ...
   much as she escaped her own
shipwrecks to swim ashore,
   leaving behind splinterings

of past pirated lives. Gazing across
　　water trails and high grasses
at descendants, she feels how feral
　　she is, body drifting

with other tidal bodies.
　　Sun plunges vermilion, sunrays
sole riders on reddening
　　backs. More than anything
she loves the manes spilling down
　　one side, streaming over necks
bowing to sedge grass and rose mallow,
　　making her grateful her own hair
flows long. O that foal prancing her way,
　　tossing wild mane … the filly, the flame.

# Blueberry Picking (for Erelene, Karin & Michelle)

After I returned from roving abroad,
August had come to the Catskills …
and the Moon for blueberry picking
with my sister and women friends.
The first day we got kicked out
of a blueberry patch I loved long ago,
rich city slickers owned it now
and one of those rough country gals
worked as their cop. What a shame,
we agreed, to become like that …

then drove away until I suggested
we check the crest of a high hill where
my mate owned land, and, damn,
that height was what its neighbors
named Blueberry Heaven on a painted sign
near the borderline, having borrowed
the patch for their own picking pleasure …
so we pulled over to enter in
with our happy pails and summer sun
spinning halos from our hair

while eight hands reached for various
blues of berries like tiny circles of sky
containing all life's sweetness ripening
from flower to fruit in a swirl of bees
not yet extinct. We gatherers

gave thanks among bushes buzzing
and green-gleaming, I recalling
my May pilgrimage to Skara Brae
on the Bay of Skaill, Neolithic
village five thousand years old,

far inside my bones feeling the ones
no longer here except at the borderline
of dream, longing for the lost equality
Orkney people embraced in that place
where the Selkies still swam to land
to shed seal skins and mate with men,
creating mythic daughters like these
weaving through bushes that much later
the Perseids would for an instant light up
in night mountains shaped like bears

whose scat appears near the plumpest
blueberries drooping off branches
caressing Mother Earth. Oh, to be
Skara Brae's sea-graced islanders
who had no weapons, who made instead
mystery carvings breathless in stone.
We gatherers filled our pails in a drift
of ancestress silence, occasionally
crushing blueberries on awed tongues
tasting an ancient wine.

# Lately, I Identify

Lately, I identify as a fire opal,
quiet and round in my October
birth month, woman whose
skin and hair have lightened up
to opal white, spirit flashing
glints of former fire mirroring
Catskill trees encircling me
with gold, vermilion, orange.

I like to imagine the tiny flames
are all the other identities
I embraced before this one,
awed zygote, baby girl,
tomboy, "part Indian" rebel,
green-eyed flower child,
peace activist, feminist, wife,
ex-wife, professor, writer, rover,

the list could blaze on. Not
that I desired to identify
with anything after my dawn
birth, but once the family doctor
swung my nakedness upside down,
slapped me into my first bawl,
the humans who named me
expected Susan to create

an accompaniment of identity.
For over six decades I strove
to compose that music equaling
a do-re-mi of me, sing myself
to a world demanding a label.
Friends, I shake my long wisdom hair
loose and bequeath all the identities
and fighting over identity to you

now that I have lightened up, this opal
of soft little fires simple in mountains.

# Woman in Wood, Skulptur by Beat Stähli

Woman liberated from tree by the woodcarver's hands ...
      Dryad curves and hollows polished to softest sheen.
The woman's hungry hip, lonely hand, bare foot
      pressed to Mother Earth ... flowing with grain

and whorls of interior wood.  How holy her hair
      weaving root-like into mountain land ... unbound
as first ancestress' long hair ... buried beauty until
      Swiss wood sculptor heard her heartbeat

beneath bark, his own Eagle heart flying to locked
      spirit whose muteness called to him louder
than any wail. Nude carved loose from dark,
      still dreaming, gleaming awake from the eternity

of patience the woodcarver's blade promised
      would be as a Tree of Life. Lady of wood
coaxed into love so sensuous, tender, fiery, wild,
      that upon seeing it other women weep,

beholding ancestresses in her ... all their migrations,
      all their joy and grief ... feeling made love to
in the way they needed a god's wakening touch.
      O dance of atoms, O woman of elusive face

evoked by Green Man carver whose eyes glint
      with forest vision, hair curling Bacchus-black ...
artist untamed, wine-kissed mouth still smiling
      despite secret pain, angst over what isn't free.

Skulptur given life by the seer who radiant dwells
        near Lake Brienz ... shadow on one side of Alps,
on Beat's side hands of light. And I, like edelweiss ...
        dreaming in the hemisphere of night.

Beat Stähli ist 1970 in Brienz – Schweiz geboren und aufgewachsen. Als vierte Generation der bekannten Holzbildhauerfamilie Stähli erhielt er in seiner frühesten Jugend Einblick in die bildende Kunst. 1987-91 folgte das Studium an der Schule für Bildhauerei in Brienz. Seit nun fünfundzwanzig Jahren ist der Bildhauer Beat Stähli als Künstler in seiner Berufung tätig.

Nach der Ausbildung lebte und arbeitete er dreieinhalb Jahre mit seiner Familie in Odense, Dänemark, unterhielt ein Atelier und war als Ausnahmekünstler an der Kunstakademie Odense vom Abteilungsleiter für Kunst Ingvar Cronhammer eingeladen, ein Atelier in der Akademie zu führen. Seit 1995 lebt und arbeitet der Künstler wieder in Brienz.

Inspiriert von der zauberhaften Natur des magischen Brienzersees schuf Stähli viele bedeutende Skulpturen, die in der ganzen Welt ihre Bestimmung gefunden haben. Lebensgrosse Skulpturen in Nussbaumholz von namhaften deutschen Politikern wurden in neuerer Zeit realisiert. Zurzeit arbeitet Stähli an Porträts von zwei europäischen Staatspräsidenten.

Die Künstlerische Arbeit umfasst die klassische Bildhauerei von Menschen und Tierskulpturen, die Kunst des Zeichnens, des Modellierens und das Verfassen von lyrischen Gedichten. Stähli's Inspirationsquelle ist in der Tiefe der Schöpfung angelegt, in der Quelle des geistigen Formens seelischer Natur. Einblick in die Schönheit der Dinge, der Klang und das Schwingen der Natur und das Sein des Menschen im Kontext der Philosophie, Psychologie und Religion, wiederspiegelt das Verständnis, das Formen und Gestalten von Stähli's Schaffen. Mimik und Gestik in expressiver Haltung der Gebärden sowie impressionistische Seelenzustände finden in Stähli's Werk auf höchster ästhetisch empfundener Ebene eindrucksvolle Wiedergabe.

Sein - Beat Stähli

Was immer war, was immer ist,
das Sein, das alles spricht.
Im jetzt und nur im jetzt entspringt.
Die Kraft der Seele zum Geiste dringt.

Beat Stähli (1970-) was born and raised in Brienz, a lakeside town in the Swiss Alps. A fourth generation member of the famous woodcarver family Stähli, in early youth Beat already possessed insight into the visual arts and expressed a gift for drawing and sculpting. From 1987-1991, he studied at the School of Wood Sculpting in Brienz and, for over twenty-five years since, has been a professional woodcarver.

After his training, he lived for three and a half years with his family in Odense, Denmark, where he maintained a studio and, as an exceptional artist at the Art Academy Odense, was invited by Head of the Art Department, Ingvar Cronhammer, to lead his own studio within the school. In 1995, the artist returned to Brienz, where he currently lives and works.

Inspired by the enchanting natural magic of Lake Brienz and surrounding Alps, he has carved many prominent sculptures, most recently life-size ones in walnut wood of German politicians. A few of the locations where his works reside are in the Federal Palace of Switzerland in Bern, in the office of Federal Councillor Ueli Maurer, and the Swiss National Museum in Zurich. Other sculptures have found a place with private collectors in London, Houston and Las Vegas, and a longtime friend and patron in Interlaken. Currently the artist is working on portraits of two European presidents.

Beat Stähli's artistic work includes classic sculptures of humans and animals, drawings, modeling, and lyric poems. Stähli's source of inspiration resides in the depths of creation, the source where our emotional nature is spiritually molded. His insight into the beauty of things, the sounds and vibrations of nature, and the essence of human beings in the context of philosophy, psychology and religion, are reflected in the design, formation, and execution of Stähli's work. Facial expressions and gestures in body attitude and impressionistic Seelenzustande (state of soul) pervade his sculptures at the most sensitive level of aesthetic perception, conveying radiant insight into the human heart, the wondrous complexity of existence, and those wilder mysteries that can only evoke wordless awe.


Kunst - Beat Stähli

Es zieht mich immer wieder mit Liebe hin.
Das alles ist des einen göttlichen sin.
Wo der Geist und die Kunst zusammen flanieren,
wird die Seele mit dem Herzen das Höchste kreieren.

Susan Deer Cloud, a mixed lineage Catskill Indian, is an alumna of Goddard College (MFA) and Binghamton University (B.A. and M.A.). She has taught Creative Writing, Rhetoric and Literature at Binghamton University and Broome Community College. A few years ago she returned to her "heart country" Catskills to dwell once more with foxes, deer, black bears, bald eagles, and the ghosts of panthers and ancestors. She now lives as a full-time mountain woman, dreamer and writer.

Deer Cloud is the recipient of various awards and fellowships, including an Elizabeth George Foundation Grant, a National Endowment for the Arts Literature Fellowship, two New York State Foundation for the Arts Fellowships, and a Chenango County Council for the Arts Individual Artist's Grant. Some of her books are *Hunger Moon* (Shabda Press); *Fox Mountain*, *The Last Ceremony* and *Car Stealer* (FootHills Publishing); and *Braiding Starlight* (Split Oak Press). Her poems, stories and essays have been published in anthologies and journals too numerous to name.

In order to get out "the voices of the voiceless," the poet has edited three published anthologies: multicultural *Confluence* and Native American anthologies *I Was Indian (Before Being Indian Was Cool), Volumes I & II*; the 2008 Spring Issue of *Yellow Medicine Review, a Journal of Indigenous Literature, Art & Thought*; and the Re-Matriation Chapbook Series of Indigenous Poetry. She is a member of the international peace organization SERVAS; Poets & Writers; Associated Writing Programs (AWP); and indigenous Wordcraft Circle. She has served on panels at writers' conferences and given myriad poetry readings at colleges, cultural centers, coffee houses, and other venues.

In between her sojourns in the Catskills, Deer Cloud has spent the past few years roving with her life's companion, John Gunther, around Turtle Island (North America) as well as on the Isles (Iceland, Ireland, Scotland, Wales and England) and Europe. She has been not only on a physical journey but a spiritual quest for her deepest roots tied in with ancestresses, ancient truths, and the sacred web of life. One magical part of this journey was meeting Beat Stähli, the cover artist for *Before Language*, who she has come to consider both a mountain brother and kindred spirit. She a daughter of the Catskill Mountains, he the son of the Swiss Alps, she views their creative collaboration as a friendship dreaming the two halves of the world together into a wholeness embodying peace and love.

www.ingramcontent.com/pod-product-compliance
Lightning Source LLC
Chambersburg PA
CBHW020538050525
26156CB00008BA/159